PAKISTAN CRISIS

BY DAVID LOSHAK

McGraw-Hill Book Company
New York   St. Louis   San Francisco
Düsseldorf   Mexico

V

ML '72 0 3 1 9 2
84 0977

First Edition

Loshak, David.
    Pakistan Crisis.

    1. Pakistan—Politics and government.   I.   Title.
DS384.L67 1972   320.9'549'04   71–38934
ISBN 0–07–038752–4

CONTENTS

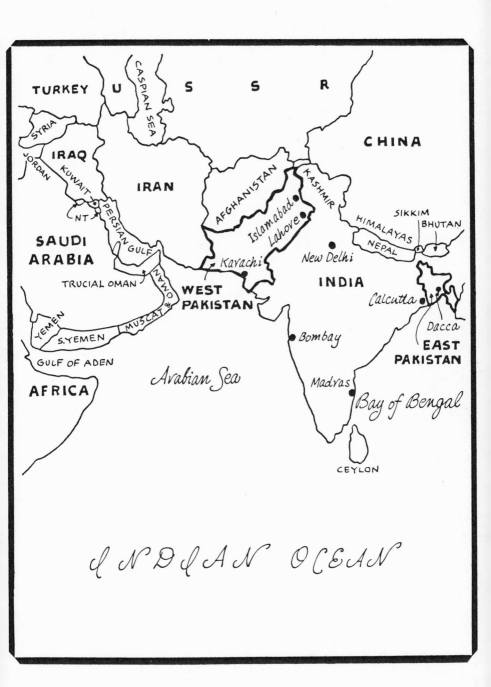

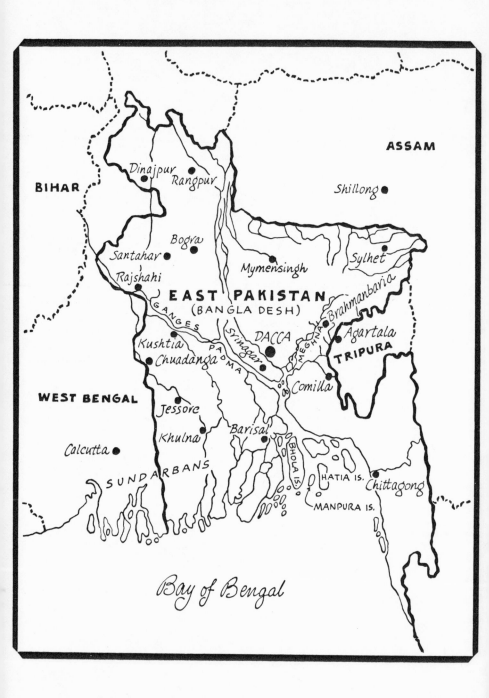

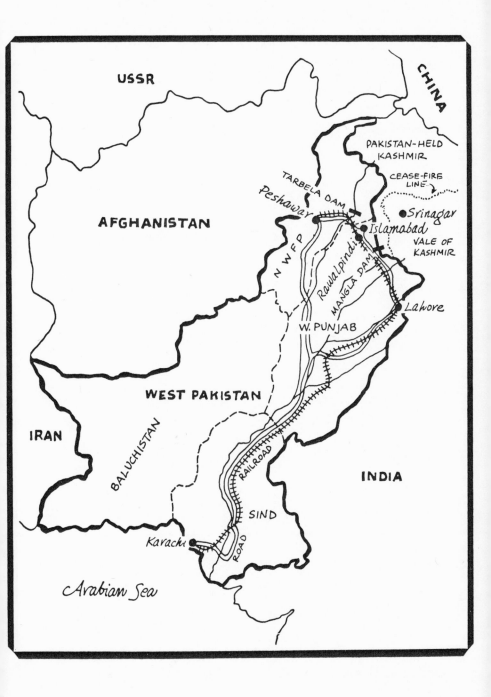

PREFACE

This book has had to be written speedily in uncloistered conditions of a kind which would appall an academic but in which, fortunately, newspapermen can thrive—hotel bedrooms without benefit of files, the living-room table surrounded by an only intermittently respectful family, in snatched moments between planes and meals. Also, it is not an academic book. This certainly does not mean that I have played fancy-free with facts, but it does mean that I have left many details of ephemeral significance to the Ph.D. theses, in the interest of the general reader. I expect the book will therefore outrage many in India and Britain who are more knowledgeable than I about Partition, for example, and who have personal memories of it. (Readers in Pakistan will almost certainly not be annoyed—the opportunity will be denied them by the censors, unless they are fed carefully edited extracts.) I am, of course, very conscious of the book's deficiencies. My main aim, however, has been to write for those who are interested in and concerned about what is going on in Pakistan and do not, perhaps, know as much as they would wish about it. If, in doing this, I have offended the purists and pundits, I am sorry, but to have satisfied them would have meant writing a book of narrower scope. Some facts, furthermore, have proved beyond precise verification: official Pakistan figures on such matters as defense, or development expenditure in the East wing, are unreliable or even "cooked." Neutral sources, such as the World Bank and other agencies, often conflict. In such cases, my aim has always been to describe trends rather than provide hard and fast textbook statistics.

Opinions, of course, are another matter. I do not apologize for mine at all. Very few other outside, neutral observers have seen the latest phases of Pakistan's disintegration at first hand throughout the crucial phases since the downfall of Ayub. Also, I have had the advantage of being a journalist. Journalists, of course, are rather despised by the various kinds of "expert" one meets- -professional apologists, bureaucrats, and sundry ax-grinders. But as a reporter I have not suffered the inhibitions and restraints which have hampered even the ablest of the few Western diplomats in Pakistan during this period. The quality of much senior diplomatic assessment in Pakistan of the scene there, on which the very ambivalent present policies toward Pakistan are partly based, was exposed in its full, inglorious, and chronic inadequacy during the aftermath of the cyclone disaster of November 1970. Journalists, for all their supposed faults, would and did do better than this as a matter of the day's work. Indeed, it was the press, radio, and television which alerted the world to the magnitude of the catastrophe and prepared it for the even greater political disasters which followed. Meanwhile, the "statesmen," cocooned in a world of their own, continue on the apparent principles that might is right and what is, stays. This, presumably, accounts for their squalid efforts to curry favor with the thoroughly discredited and blood-smeared regime in Islamabad, while innocents die and suffer by the million.

Not that this book will make the slightest difference to that. You can't beat *real-politik*. But what I hope it may do is to clarify the main developments and problems of Pakistan—a muddied and muddling story. Although a little-known and little-understood nation, Pakistan is no less important for that: it is, after all, the fifth largest nation in the world and China's close ally. I first realized, with shock, how deep the gap is between Eastern facts and Western understanding in a conversation during 1970 with a distinguished British visitor to India—a household name in Britain, Europe, and the United States. He scarcely even realized that India and Pakistan were

separate countries. He certainly lacked the faintest idea of
what it would involve to tackle Pakistan's problems. Despite
his scientific training, for example, he suggested to me that the
"solution" to East Pakistan's overpopulation problem would
be to move the "extra people" round somehow to West
Pakistan—thereby begging host of enormous economic, social
and political questions that should have sprung to the mind of
anyone purporting to be informed, quite apart from the impossible logistics of the exercise. So I hope this book fills such
gaps of knowledge and understanding. Suddenly, Pakistan has
become big news, thousands send money and goods to its
cruelly fated people, and worry about the latest world trouble
spot. So it might not be a bad thing if they knew and understood a little more about it.

I am sure there is no one who particularly wishes to be
publicly associated with this book. But many have been
associated, perhaps unwittingly. I owe special thanks to fellow
journalists in India and Pakistan (those in the latter country I
could not name as it would endanger their livelihood if not
their lives). I am indebted to diplomatic friends who have
made Pakistan their special study only to be ignored by their
superiors at home. I have unashamedly picked the brains of
professional men and civil servants in Pakistan, among whom
many of those who are Bengalis have been butchered, perse-
cuted, or condemned to exile. The *Daily Telegraph* and *Sunday Telegraph,* for whom I have been staff correspondent in
South Asia, have given me admirable opportunities to travel
widely and learn about Pakistan in some depth. Mr. Robert
Sykes, late of the British Council in Dacca, gave me insights
into the situation on the basis of his formidable personal
knowledge of East Pakistan, its people and its leaders. For
finally dissolving my sloth and moving me into getting the
book written I thank my brother-in-law, Dr. Charles Feinstein,
senior tutor of Clare College, Cambridge, and James Cameron,
a great journalist, good friend, and continual inspiration. But
most deep-felt gratitude goes to Mollie, my wife, who has
steadfastly endured the many uncompensated deprivations and
vexations of being married to a compulsive journalist.

Acknowledgments are due to Reuters Ltd. for permission to

quote from a report by Mr. Maurice Quaintance; The *Daily Telegraph* Ltd. for permission to quote from reports by Mr. Simon Dring and Mrs. Jill Knight, M.P.; *Times Newspapers Ltd.* for permission to use extracts from a report by Mr. Anthony Mascaranhas which appeared in the *Sunday Times;* and the *New Statesman* for permission to quote from an article by Mr. Reg Prentice, M.P.

CHRONOLOGY

1930: The idea of "Pakistan," a separate home for Muslims to be carved out of India after independence, first proposed, by President of Muslim League.

1933: Choudri Rahmat Ali coins the name "Pakistan," meaning "land of the spiritually pure and clean" in Urdu. Its letters taken from the names of the Muslim homelands in the subcontinent.

August 15, 1947: Pakistan attains independence. M. A. Jinnah, Muslim League president, becomes governor-general; Liaquat Ali Khan prime minister.

October 19, 1947: War with India over Kashmir.

September 11, 1948: Jinnah dies.

July 26, 1949: Kashmir cease-fire agreed to under United Nations supervision. Kashmir divided along cease-fire line pending a settlement which never came.

October 16, 1951: Liaquat Ali Khan murdered.

October 7, 1958: Army takes over in bloodless *coup d'état*. Ayub Khan becomes president. Martial law.

October 26, 1959: Ayub announces scheme for "basic democracy."

March 1, 1962: Ayub signs constitution.

June 8, 1962: New assembly of "basic democrats" meets. Martial law lifted.

September 6, 1965: Full-scale war with India breaks out in Kashmir. State of Emergency regulations.

September 23, 1965: Cease-fire.

January 10, 1966: Tashkent agreement.

March 20, 1966: President Ayub denounces autonomist movement in East Pakistan.

January 6, 1968: Government launches Agartala conspiracy case against Sheikh Mujibur Rahman and thirty-four others.

October 10, 1968: Students launch antigovernment agitation.

November 7, 1968: Assassination attempt on President Ayub Khan.

November 13, 1968: Mr. Bhutto, former foreign minister, arrested.

November 17, 1968: Air Marshal Asghar Khan denounces President Ayub.

December 1, 1968: President Ayub agrees to most of student demands but agitation continues.

December 7, 1968: Disorder spreads to East Pakistan.

December 30, 1968: President Ayub agrees to accept only "genuine and beneficial" amendments to constitution.

January 8, 1969: Opposition leaders call for end of "one-man dictatorship." Issue series of fundamental demands. Disorder mounts.

February 1, 1969: President Ayub agrees to discuss any constitutional changes.

February 14, 1969: Nationwide general strike.

February 17, 1969: Emergency regulations lifted nearly three and a half years after end of Kashmir war. East Pakistan unappeased; rioting spreads.

February 21, 1969: President Ayub announces decision not to stand for reelection.

February 22, 1969: Agartala conspiracy case abandoned.

March 13, 1969: President Ayub agrees after three-day talks (now generally known as the "R.T.C."—Round Table Conference) with Bhutto, Mujib, and other leaders to parliamentary government and direct elections. Mass strikes and disturbances continue. Mujib takes initiative in ending East Pakistan anarchy.

March 23–24, 1969: Troops move in to guard all main installations and vital points.

March 25, 1969: President Ayub Khan resigns. General

Yahya Khan, commander in chief, takes over. Martial law. Order quickly restored.

March 26, 1969: In nationwide broadcast, President Yahya disclaims any political ambition and promises restoration of civilian government.

April 10, 1969: President Yahya declares that on the question of East Pakistan's autonomy, "It is entirely for the elected representatives of the people to decide what they want."

April–July, 1969: President Yahya holds series of talks with leading politicians.

July 28, 1969: President Yahya promises general election within 18 months. Declares dissatisfaction in East Pakistan "fully justified."

August 4, 1969: Ten civilian cabinet ministers, including five from East Pakistan, sworn in.

November 28, 1969: President Yahya gives October 5, 1970, as general election date. One-man, one-vote basis. Built-in majority for East Pakistan, but provincial autonomy must be consistent with strong federal government at center.

December 2, 1969: Air Marshal Asghar Khan announces retirement from politics as all his aims have been fulfilled by President Yahya.

January 1, 1970: Political restrictions lifted; parties resume full activity.

March 28, 1970: Legal Framework Order gives detailed blueprint for return to civilian government.

August 16, 1970: General election postponed until December 7 due to widespread flooding in East Pakistan.

November 12, 1970: Cyclone kills estimated 500,000 in East Pakistan and causes immense destruction over wide area.

November 26, 1970: Sheikh Mujib denounces West Pakistan for callous disregard of East wing's sufferings.

November 27, 1970: President Yahya defends his government as having "done its damnedest" to help cyclone survivors.

November 28, 1970: Pope Paul visits Dacca.

December 7, 1970: Pakistan's first one-man, one-vote election gives sweeping victory to Sheikh Mujibur Rahman's Awami League in East Pakistan and Mr. Z. A. Bhutto's People's Party in West Pakistan.

December 15, 1970: Bhutto says new Constitution must preserve Pakistan's integrity, solidarity, and unity.

December 17, 1970: Provincial election results confirm general election. President Yahya describes Mujib as "Pakistan's next prime minister." National Assembly to meet in
early March 1971.

December 20, 1970: Mujib refuses to budge from Six-Point
Program.

December 27, 1970: Bhutto threatens to withdraw from constitution-making process.

January 17, 1971: Awami League wins all nine cyclone-
affected constituencies where voting was deferred, giving it
a total of 160 in assembly of 300 plus seven out of 13
women's seats.

February 17, 1971: Bhutto says attending assembly "pointless" because of Mujib's "inflexibility."

February 21, 1971: President Yahya dismisses civilian cabinet.

February 22, 1971: President Yahya convenes meeting of
military governors as crisis begins to deepen.

March 1, 1971: Assembly meeting postponed "indefinitely."

March 2, 1971: Mujib calls general strike in Dacca, which
spreads to whole of East Pakistan. Beginning of a week of
disruption.

March 3, 1971: President Yahya invites all political leaders to
round-table conference. Mujib rejects invitation.

March 6, 1971: President Yahya refixes Assembly convening
for March 25 but comes near to challenging East wing to
showdown.

March 7, 1971: Sheikh Mujib holds back from expected
declaration of an independent Bangla Desh. Announces
civil-disobedience movement. Refuses to attend Assembly
unless President Yahya agrees to series of preconditions.

March 9, 1971: Foreigners begin evacuation from East
Pakistan.

March 15, 1971: President Yahya arrives in Dacca for talks
with Sheikh Mujib.

March 16–20, 1971: Secret talks between Yahya and Mujib
produce a shaky compromise.

March 22, 1971: Bhutto joins talks, which collapse. Inaugural assembly again postponed.

March 23, 1971: Pakistan's "Republic Day" becomes "Resistance Day" in East Pakistan.

March 25, 1971: Yahya and Bhutto leave Dacca. Mujib arrested. Army launches mass attack on Awami League, students, Hindus, and Bengalis generally. Bengali elements in army and police mutiny.

March 26, 1971: President Yahya denounces Sheikh Mujib as a traitor, bans Awami League and issues stiff new series of martial law directives. Rigorous clampdown on reporting of developments inside East Pakistan.

April 16, 1971: Army attains grip on all of East Pakistan.

April 17, 1971: Bangla Desh "government" of Awami Leaguers takes office at "Mujibnagar."

April 21, 1971: 259,000 East Pakistani refugees announced by India.

April 22, 1971: U Thant offers relief on solely humanitarian grounds.

May 3, 1971: President Yahya says there is no cause for humanitarian concern.

May 19, 1971: Refugee figure tops 3,000,000.

May 21, 1971: President Yahya says "bona fide" Pakistan citizens should come home.

May 24, 1971: Mrs. Gandhi tells Indian parliament that there are no "military solutions." After accusations and counteraccusations of border violations, Pakistan charges India with interfering in her internal affairs.

June 11, 1971: India announces plans for dispersing refugees, but these were to prove ineffective.

June 17, 1971: Lieutenant General Tikka Khan appeals to refugees to return home, sets up reception centers and offers an amnesty.

June 20, 1971: Mr. Jagjivan Ram, defense minister, says India is prepared for any eventuality.

June 26, 1971: Mr. M. M. Ahmed, President Yahya's chief economic adviser, says Pakistan spending 56 per cent of budget on defense.

June 28, 1971: President Yahya, in nationwide broadcast, says Constitution will be prepared by experts and based on the people's aspirations as assessed by him. Admits economy shattered. Hopes to achieve transfer of power within "four months or so."

June 29, 1971: Mr. Bhutto demands lifting of ban on political activity.

July 8, 1971: Refugee figure reaches 6,700,000 according to Indian sources.

July 12, 1971: World Bank report on East Pakistan.

July 15, 1971: United States says value of its arms sent to Pakistan only $2,200,000. House of Representatives foreign affairs committee votes to cut off economic as well as military aid to Pakistan.

July 19, 1971: President Yahya threatens to declare war on India.

August 9, 1971: Indo-Soviet 20-year treaty, India's first major pact with military overtones.

August 13, 1971: U Thant says refugee figure now 7,500,000.

August 22, 1971: Bangla Desh guerillas sink four ships in Chittagong. Guerilla campaign of destruction mounts.

September 3, 1971: Mr. Abdul Motaleb Malik appointed as "puppet" governor of East Pakistan: appointment dismissed as "eyewash" by Mr. Bhutto.

September 4, 1971: Lieutenant General Tikka Khan removed to become corps commander in West Pakistan along key stretch of frontier with India. General amnesty announced, but many prisoners (including Sheikh Mujib) not released.

September 17, 1971: East Pakistan "cabinet" of ten members sworn in.

September 19, 1971: Election commission gives new timetable. By-elections for 79 disqualified Awami League national assembly members to be held between November 25 and December 9.

October 10, 1971: Total ban on political activity lifted; stringent curbs remain.

October 12, 1971: President Yahya says new assembly will meet on December 27. Will have power to amend Constitution, to be published before December 20, subject to his approval.

October 15, 1971: U.S. Senate foreign relations committee votes to cut off all aid to Pakistan.

October 20, 1971: Pakistan military build-up in Punjab completed; Indian military preparations reach advanced stage.

October 24, 1971: Mrs. Gandhi, Indian prime minister, begins three-week tour of Western capitals in attempt to increase international pressure on Pakistan.

INTRODUCTION

"Joi Bangla," "Joi Bangla," "Joi Bangla": this was the chant on a million lips at a vast rally in Dacca, capital of East Pakistan, on March 7, 1971. "Joi Bangla" means, in Bengali, "Victory to Bengal." That "victory" was the dream which brought so many excited, wide-and-wild-eyed men of every age (and even some women—a rare sight beyond the home in Muslim Dacca) to the enormous throng that sunny Sunday. They came to hear their great hero and political leader, Sheikh Mujibur Rahman, declare the breakaway and long-yearned-for independence of their land from the oppression by their fellow nationals and fellow Muslims in West Pakistan. They expected to witness that day the birth of a new Bengali nation, or "Bangla Desh."

Many had walked twenty, fifty, even more miles, barefoot and with little food, to hear the Sheikh. Rarely can so many hopes have been so swiftly, so cruelly dashed. It was not Mujib (as Sheikh Mujibur Rahman was popularly known) who disappointed them, though he did not in fact declare an independent "Bangla Desh." He stopped short of that brink but contrived, by dint of the brilliant crowd oratory of which he was a master, to send the masses away enthused and, for the time, content, believing that independence was around the corner. But in under a month, the Bengali people of East Pakistan were beneath the vicious heel of West Pakistan militarism as never before: Soon tens of thousands were dead, hundreds of thousands starving, millions were fleeing their homeland. Mujib himself was incarcerated awaiting an uncertain fate, publicly charged with high treason. And ruin and despair, the utter antithesis to the mood of that heady and euphoric Sunday, were symbolized by the pathetic corpses left to rot on the very spot where Sheikh Mujib had held the multitude spellbound. In the summer of 1971, green Bengal ran red.

The dreadful compulsions which led the military leaders of West Pakistan to slaughter Bengalis in their thousands and to wage a campaign of terrorism against them, which led Bengalis to wreak indiscriminate vengeance with equally unsparing cruelty, which set Bengali against Bengali, which led the masses of East Pakistan to revolt repeatedly and with growing violence against their government, which brought fellow Muslims owing allegiance to the same flag into one of the bitterest, most savage conflicts of recent times, which sent more than ten million terrified and impoverished people fleeing for their lives to a new living death in the squalid refugee camps of India—all this is the story of this book.

Pakistan today, in its two wings, has a total population of 136 million people—less the ten million or so estimated to have fled to India, and less also the uncounted thousands massacred by the army in the names of "national integrity" and Allah. But even at 125 millions Pakistan has the fifth largest population in the world, after China, India, the United States and Soviet Russia. It is also vitally placed in terms of international power politics. It is of key concern to the two major Asian powers, Russia and China, and also, therefore, to the United States. It is not an exaggeration to say that what happens in Pakistan matters to the world as a whole. This is in a purely political and strategic sense: there are, of course, the moral issues which are also involved in Pakistan's plight and which are of equal concern—or should be—whatever the political aspects. If those come second here, it is only because it is that order of priorities which unhappily obtains in world affairs.

The key to the problems of Pakistan is its irrevocable division into two widely separate parts, divided from each other by about 1,000 miles of India. Fundamentally, the real wonder is not that Pakistan is now a nation in such deep crisis but that it has lasted so long without breaking up. For Pakistan was doomed from the start.

A century ago, perhaps even more recently, this might not have mattered much to the world beyond. With that "realistic" lack of moral sense which has almost always determined foreign policies, we would have let Pakistan stew in its own juice. But that is no longer possible or, at any rate, practical. Those same reasons of self-interest compel faraway countries to do something about Pakistan, to take some positive decisions about it, or take instead the risk of unpleasant long-term consequences. What some of these might be are outlined in the later chapters. So far, Western governments have shown little sign that they understand the nature and causes of Pakistan's problems, and even less sign that they have any worthwhile ideas about solving them. And I believe this is a matter for more than mere disquiet. For in East Pakistan the world truly confronts, for the first time, the ultimate fulfillment of the Malthusian nightmare—the prediction by the eighteenth-century economist that population would eventually outstrip the world's food supply and other resources and even living space. That stage has been reached in East Pakistan, where the sheer weight of population—helped by special factors which derive from Pakistan's division into two—has gravely damaged, perhaps irreparably destroyed, the very fabric of an entire society. And while Pakistan may be unique in its particular problems, the crisis of population is a world problem. So one returns to the point: The world must note what has happened. "It can't happen here" has always been a stupid solace of a slogan. Never more so than now. The direct result of Pakistan's disintegration, not a sudden "happening" but the result of a process which began long ago and *was* foreseen, as the published records prove, is the mass human tragedy enacted in the summer of 1971 by six million refugees in the hot, wet, foetid camps of Indian Bengal and by millions more who did not escape from "Bangla Desh." It need not be the only result.

1

PARTITION OF INDIA

India in March 1947 was a ship on fire in midocean with ammunition in the hold.—LORD MOUNTBATTEN

Pakistan was a nation born in a hurry. It came to life as it has since subsisted and is now expiring: in crisis and carnage. It was an ill-fated nation. In a real sense, it was never a nation at all, and this has been its pathetic fallacy, its downfall.

Pakistan was born out of the partition of India in 1947. After the Second World War, Britain began the great pull-out from her vast overseas empire, of which the largest and richest jewel was India—the great subcontinental mass which stretched from the desert borders of Persia in the west, nearly 2,000 miles across to the tropical jungles of the Burmese frontier, from the Himalayas to within eight degrees of the equator.

It was a land of enormous diversity. It had a multiplicity of languages and customs, deep poverty and immense wealth, peoples of every kind and degree, and, most crucially of all, two dominant and utterly contrasting religions. These were Hinduism, the faith that regards the cow as holy and is deeply rooted in thousands of years of India's history, and the faith of the Muslims, who believe in the divinity of the prophet Muhammad of Islam. It was the irreconcilability of these two creeds which led, in 1947, to the division of India into two separate sovereign nations, India and Pakistan.

It was not until very late in the process of quitting India that its British overlords decided on "partition," decided, that is, on creating these two new nations. When Britain, under Mr. Attlee's Labour government, began the process, a major aim was to preserve India's unity. But this proved impossible when cleavages between Muslim and Hindu grew too great. An all-India interim government which was set up in the autumn of 1946 under Mr. Nehru, a Hindu (even if not a practicing or orthodox Hindu), signaled the start of a sixteen-month communal bloodbath, and the slaughter and chaos which ensued right along the 1,500-mile belt of the Indo-Gangetic plain compelled Britain to quit far more rapidly than planned. Pressure relentlessly mounted so that in February 1947 Britain undertook to leave within fifteen months. Simultaneously, the thrusting and dynamic Lord Mountbatten took over as viceroy from the placid, contemplative, more wise but less decisive Wavell. But, as the civil war intensified and spread, even that express timetable was jettisoned. On June 4 Mountbatten delivered the stunning announcement that Britain would decamp in a mere eleven weeks. And not only that: the once great empire would be dismantled, "partitioned," and a new nation, Pakistan, would be born.

And so it was. The idea of Pakistan, however, was far from new. The word itself was coined in 1933; it is composed of letters from the names of the Islamic homelands: Punjab, Afghania (that is, the northwest frontier region of old India), Kashmir, Iran, Sind, Turkharistan, Afghanistan, and Baluchistan. Not all these areas have become parts of Pakistan as it is today: even more significantly, the region which now composes East Pakistan, which is a crucial part of Pakistan's identity, is not included either. But it was an idea, and this basic idea remained: to create a nation where the 100 million Muslims then living on the subcontinent could develop their own way of life free from the domination of the Hindus, who outnumbered them three to one.

In contrast to India, a secular state, not based, despite its Hindu majority, on the Hindu religion, Pakistan was founded on the basis of a religious aspiration, to provide a homeland for the Muslims of the Indian subcontinent. Its basis, its core, its very being, is Islamic.

The irreconcilability of Muslim and Hindu goes back centuries. As religions, they differ deeply. Islam is, like Christianity, monotheistic and lays stress on the basic equality of human beings before the law and its God, Allah. Hinduism, in contrast, has many gods or, at any rate, a flexible attitude to the concept of God, and in its caste system positively exalts, exploits, and perpetuates supposedly immutable human inequalities. Hinduism is a faith rooted in, almost synonymous with, the land of India, or Holy Mother India as the Indians regard it. Islam, however, came to the subcontinent as an alien, invading force, starting in the eighth century, and it brought (as well as the finest products of a great civilization, including the Taj Mahal) immense death and destruction. For nearly six hundred years, Muslim kings and emperors kept large parts of India in thrall. It was an historical heritage which inevitably and deeply rankled.

It led to more than a religious cleft: there is a wide cultural gap between the Hindu and Muslim too. It is very noticeable today in the contrast between the muddled, inefficient, even dirty way in which the typical Indian town—or even Delhi, the capital—is run, and the relatively westernized, more concerned way in which a city like Karachi operates. Karachi is no great city, to be sure, but whereas in the great decaying cities of the West, like New York, one finds, in Galbraith's phrase, "private affluence and public squalor," in Karachi, Pakistan's largest city, there is, according to its lights, private squalor and public affluence, while in the typical Indian city one finds private squalor and public squalor. The comparative westernization of many Pakistanis, as compared, that is, with their Indian counterparts, is in part an Islamic heritage, and it is part of what sets the Muslim apart from, and makes him distrusted, feared, or envied by, the Hindu.

And Islam, like Hinduism, is more than a religion. Both are codes of living which affect everything important and even much that is not important in life. And this, of course, exacerbates their incompatibility.

The Hindus worship the cow; Muslims eat it: a difference which has led to bloody communal riots in the subcontinent year after year. As Mr. Jinnah, the "father" of Pakistan, once pointed out, Muslim attitudes not only differ from but clash with Hindu ideals. Muslim and Hindu history and heroes, art and architecture and music, names and clothing and diets and humor, their attitudes toward women and children, toward personal hygiene, toward burial and cremation, toward marriage and education—all contrast sharply.

In the last century of British India, the Muslims found themselves not only a minority, and a very different, almost alien minority at that, but very much second-class citizens. This largely stemmed from the time of the Indian Mutiny in 1857, which led to much unjustifiable victimization of the Muslim community. The Muslims were being rudely displaced from their former hegemony, and they felt it. Hindu-Muslim cooperation in the anti-British independence movement under the leadership of Gandhi flourished briefly in the 1920s, but, for a variety of complex political reasons, turned sour. Muslim concern now came to center on the problem of what their position would be in an independent India dominated by Hindus. The Hindu-dominated Congress party, which was the spearhead of the movement against Britain, and which has ruled independent India from 1947 to this day, was clearly in a position to overrule Muslim opinion and sentiment at every point. Many Hindus sincerely disclaimed any such intention; many Muslims, with equal sincerity, could not see how it would be avoided. When the prospect of independence became a reality, India's Muslims, led by Mr. Jinnah and the Muslim League, could find no way of reconciling their fears of Hindu domination within a one-nation frame. If we recall the sufferings of religious minorities in Europe and America in recent centuries, the persecution of Catholics in Britain or Puritans in the United States for example, or of Jews almost everywhere, it is perhaps easier to understand the intense antagonism between Muslims and Hindus—who differ far more from each other than do Jews and Christians. Indian leaders, particularly Hindus, bitterly opposed Partition, for they saw it not only as the ruination of the complex infrastructure, administrative and otherwise, which was the most valuable part of the British legacy, but as also a diminution of India's size and population and, therefore, power, and also, therefore, their personal power. Muslim leaders doubtless also saw the creation of a new nation in similar terms—but to their advantage. The new nation, they realized, could be their making: bigger fish in a smaller pond. The Muslims in India, furthermore, were economically weak compared with the Hindus. Pakistan "patriotism" was largely motivated not only, perhaps not even primarily, by Islamic aspirations but by the economic frustrations of a Muslim bourgeoisie permanently thwarted in its growth by the weight of Hindu "imperialism." Pakistan would provide their escape. All these varied factors contributed to the basic Hindu-Muslim clash, leading Mountbatten to recommend Partition. India, tragically, was thus divided.

2

PARTITION OF PAKISTAN

Mutilated,   motheaten,   truncated   Pakistan.—
JINNAH

But so, extraordinarily, and with equal tragedy, was Pakistan.
For the basis of Partition was that the subcontinent was to be
divided into Hindu-majority and Muslim-majority areas. And
the eastern half of the Indian state of Bengal, over on the east
of the country, was predominantly Muslim. All the other
majority Muslim states formed a contiguous area on the
country's western side and were, minus Kashmir and plus half
of the divided Punjab, to form West Pakistan. East Bengal,
quite separate, became East Pakistan—a province of Pakistan
divided by 1,000 miles of a hostile India from the rest of the
new country.

It was a partition within Partition. The Partition of India
led to immense strife and slaughter, and possibly the biggest
human migration of all time: at least half a million were killed
in the merciless communal holocaust of 1947 and 1948 and
some 14 million more were uprooted to start new lives. But
the partition of Pakistan too, creating a Pakistan divided from
its inception, was to cause enormous human suffering. And it
led directly to the upsurge in East Pakistan of 1971, which
sent a new wave of refugees, more than ten million at the latest
count and second only in size to that of 1947, surging des-

perately across the frontiers for a mite of peace and security and perhaps a respite from travail.

What, then, was the nature—or, more precisely, what were the natures—of the Pakistan, East and West, spawned by the disintegration of Britain's Indian empire?

The two wings could hardly be more different. Physically, they are total contrasts. West Pakistan is larger than Texas, or Britain and France together, 310,000 square miles, mostly desert, arid hills, and, in the north, the mountains of the Hindu Kush, the Karakoram, and the western Himalayas. Much of it is hard, harsh land of extremes of climate, with a rainfall averaging only about 55 inches annually. Its population, today about 61 million, means there is an average population density of only 197 to the square mile. One of the most popular modes of transport, outside the cities and even in them, is the camel.

You will never see a camel in East Pakistan: the commonest form of transport is the boat. And the East is different in almost every other way. It is small—55,000 square miles, or about the area of England and Wales, or Wisconsin. It is extremely populous, with well over half of Pakistan's population—75 million people in its tiny area, or 1,360 to the square mile, nearly seven times as dense as West Pakistan and probably the highest rural concentration of population in the world. While the west wing is harsh and arid, East Pakistan is almost entirely waterlogged or wet, for it is a catchment area for one of the world's greatest river-systems, the Ganges-Brahmaputra. Much of it is flooded annually. None of East Pakistan except a sliver, the Chittagong Hill Tracts near the Burmese border, rises much above sea level. The region also has heavy monsoon rains, and annual rainfall is over 200 inches in many districts. It is a hot, steamy, wet land, crisscrossed by myriad watercourses. The roads are few and poor and traveling is interrupted by long delays at ferry crossings. Road building is difficult because, in all of East Pakistan, there is hardly any stone—merely the soft, rich silt of its vast and ever-disastrously overflowing rivers. There is only one city of any size in East Pakistan—Dacca, its capital, with a population approaching 2,000,000. Otherwise, the province is almost en-

tirely rural, with towns of no special significance. West
Pakistan, however, has two of the major cities of the Indian
subcontinent: Karachi, a westernized metropolis on the coast
of the Arabian Sea, with more than 3,000,000 people, and
Lahore, once capital of the united Punjab and probably the
most elegant city in either India or Pakistan, with a population of nearly 2,000,000. In addition, the national capital,
Islamabad, is in West Pakistan. It is a smart, completely new
city built to a master plan, in the shadow of the Karakoram
foothills. It is still unfinished and some government departments
still operate in the interim capital nearby, Rawalpindi. Pakistan
thus has several "capital" cities: Karachi, its former political
capital and mercantile capital still; Lahore, capital of the most
important province in the west wing, the Punjab; Rawalpindi,
military headquarters and still the interim capital; and then
Islamabad itself. And in the East, Dacca has been designated
as Pakistan's "second" or "legislative" capital.

The people of the two contrasting wings, wheat-growing
West Pakistan and rice-growing East Pakistan, also differ
sharply—in the West, tall and lighter-skinned, in the East,
short and dark. Indeed, these two peoples have nothing in
common except Islam, and that, as the acrimonious quarrels
of the Middle East prove, counts for nothing as a cementing
force. Peoples like the martial, pushful Punjabis and the war-
rior tribesmen of Baluchistan in the West wing are a world
away in temperament, character, methods, and background
from the lackadaisical, all-talk and little-action Bengalis. The
people of the West have always fought for their lands and
lives against many invaders and, indeed, almost all of Pakistan's soldiers during its twenty-four-year life have come from
the West wing. The Bengali, by contrast, is not an easy fighter
and is readier to let life take its own course: it needs no effort
to make the lush green riverlands fertile. Except at times like
the present, when Bengalis too have had to fight for their very
existence instead of talk about it, the unremitting tropical
steaminess, with never the stimulus of a snap of cold, fresh air,
has sapped the will and produced few "abrasive" men. So,
just as Muslims and Hindus differ on so many counts, so do
the Urdu-speaking Muslims of West Pakistan differ, utterly

and decisively, from the Bengali-speaking Muslims of East Pakistan. Kipling could have been writing about Pakistan when he said that east and west never shall meet. The two Pakistans never have met, and could not. West Pakistan is of the Middle East; East Pakistan is of the Far East. They have not much more in common than, say, Vietnam and Egypt. This has been the basic flaw in the structure of Pakistan.

But these vital distinctions have been nowhere more crucial than in the economies of the two wings. From the start, East and West Pakistan have been a pair of economic invalids, and of these two weaklings East Pakistan began as the more sickly partner and has remained so, becoming relatively more frail year by year, from the moment of Partition to the present day.

Pakistan was born as a fully-fledged nation in name but lacked what is perhaps the most essential attribute of any large modern state, a strong industrial base. As it happened, almost all of the subcontinent's great resources of coal, iron, bauxite, and other minerals were on the Indian side of the Partition lines. The strongest economic concentrations were in the great ports: Bombay, Calcutta, and Madras were all in India and only Karachi, a comparatively minor and much more recently developed port, was in Pakistan. In addition, most of the go-ahead industrialists and merchants on the Pakistan side of the Partition lines were Hindus, who left for India. So Pakistan began with only a weak string of secondary industries like textiles, glass, leather and food processing and with resources that were no more than adequate. Without Kashmir, which after conflict went to India, it proved very difficult for Pakistan to develop the power resources it needed for large-scale industrialization. And, of course, the fact that the nation was physically divided was an immense economic handicap.

Partition was particularly cruel to East Pakistan. Before Partition, when Bengal was one unit, jute was a mainstay of the economy. More than three-quarters of the world's raw jute, which has a wide range of uses in the making of matting and sacks, was grown in East Bengal. Yet in East Bengal—which became East Pakistan—there was not one jute mill: all of the jute mills were in a 60-mile strip along the Hooghly River north of Calcutta. The reasons for this were partly historical, partly geographical, but the effect of Partition on East Pakistan is the important thing and can be easily seen: its main outlet for its raw jute was blocked. (The effect on West Bengal, which had the jute mills but no jute, was equally catastrophic.)

But this was not all. For apart from jute East Pakistan had, and still has, no other cash crop except tea. It needs every ounce of rice it grows—and more—for its own people. Partition cut it off from the only major port in the area, Calcutta; Partition, in fact, cut East Pakistan's economic lifelines with the outside world, and particularly with India, on which it was so economically dependent—inescapably so, given that it was almost entirely surrounded by Indian territory. East Pakistan had even less industry than West Pakistan: a few tea factories in the Sylhet district and one or two jute mills in and around Dacca was about the sum of it. This cutting off, which occurred mainly for the political reasons of West Pakistan, was the kernel of that bitter seed sowed by Partition which was to yield the even bitterer fruit of a Pakistan divided against itself. In the years after Partition, India and Pakistan failed to find a harmonious relationship; squabbling, feuding, and actual conflict between them continually broke out. Yet there was hardly a part of each nation's economy which did not depend on a harmonious relationship. Pakistan and India were economically interdependent for jute, as we have seen, but also for such products as cotton and wool, for many basic chemicals and coal, for metals and electricity and rubber, for scores of manufactured items from tractors and cement to textiles and sugar. Partition dismantled an elaborate economic infrastructure at a stroke. "Politics based on communal hatred and suspicion is systematically undoing the work of generations," wrote an Indian authority (C. N. Vakil: *Economic Consequences of Divided India,* Bombay, 1950) with great truth. And he further pointed out that such policies defied the facts of economic geography. Of the two nations born in August 1947, Pakistan was the smaller and the weaker and therefore suffered more from this defiance than India. And of the two halves of Pakistan, it was, again, the smaller and weaker which took the brunt of economic punishment.

3

BEHEST OF THE GENERALS

Pakistan is incomplete without Kashmir both territorially and ideologically.—Z. A. BHUTTO

Partition, in a nutshell, proved (in Hobbes's phrase) "poor, nasty, brutish, and short." Like any other piece of drastic emergency surgery, it was messy in the extreme. Many loose ends were left and wounds festered for years—fester still. One of these was the status of the Indian princedoms, independent states within the state. Each of the maharajahs had to make his own decision about which of the two newly independent countries, India or Pakistan, he would join, and in most princedoms this was a simple choice, governed by whichever community, Hindu or Muslim, was in the majority in each case. But the most crucial exception, as far as Indo-Pakistan relations were concerned, was the princely state of Kashmir. What happened there has bedeviled the subcontinent ever since. And it has been a problem which has deeply affected Pakistan, for it is Kashmir that has led to the policies which, as we saw in Chapter 2, have seriously warped and stunted her development.

Kashmir was a predominantly Muslim state: Hindus were outnumbered four to one, and are still. But the maharajah, an immensely wealthy potentate of doubtful quality, was a Hindu, and he acceded (Muslims say under duress) to India. In 1947, war broke out as both Pakistan and India claimed

Kashmir. The rights and wrongs of this conflict have been argued over repeatedly ever since, and gave the fledgling United Nations' Security Council a baptism if not of fire then certainly of hot air. It would take a book in itself (and there have been plenty) to sort the issues out. But the effect was this: when, after more than a year, fighting stopped, India was in possession of most of Kashmir, including the prosperous and very beautiful Vale. Pakistan, which had always regarded Kashmir as an integral part of the Partition concept (the "k" in Pakistan), held only a section, of much less value, on the principality's western side, adjoining Pakistan proper. Since then, a cease-fire line has been policed by the United Nations. Both countries still regard Kashmir as their own and are permanently poised to go to war over it.

The inclusion of most of Kashmir within India has rankled and rankled in Pakistan. For Kashmir is a prime economic prize and being without it has been a serious economic deprivation. More fundamentally, an Indian Kashmir, as Pakistanis (and, incidentally, many Kashmiris) see it, patently conflicts with the very basis on which Partition was decided—the basis, that is, of the majority community in each state. To this, the Indians have many answers, legal, constitutional, political, and moral—but the feud over Kashmir remains deadlocked.

Despite this, Kashmir has been of use to Pakistan: it gave the new nation a cause. Pakistan had no policy, no formed attitude, when it came into being: Kashmir became at once the cornerstone and the keystone of its foreign policy where there had been no foreign policy. And that foreign policy, of course, has determined defense policy. Kashmir is the chief reason why Pakistan has always maintained a large, strong army, and it is the size and influence of the army which has been the most important feature of Pakistan's political development.

But Kashmir was not all of the detritus that Partition left in its wake. Another "untidy" aspect of the process was that many Hindus stayed in Pakistan and many more Muslims remained in India. Partition was not clean-cut. India's Muslims today total some 57 million, which makes secular India the third largest Muslim nation in the world, after Indonesia and

Pakistan itself and well ahead of the Arab countries which are the seat of Islam. How many Hindus remain in Pakistan today is almost impossible to say because the available statistics, often inaccurate and usually outdated, have been made hopelessly unreliable by the anti-Hindu massacres and the flight of the refugees during 1971. But perhaps 4,000,000 remain. The point, however, is not the numbers involved, but the very fact that there are sizable Hindu and Muslim minorities in each country. This has been an ever-present bone of communal contention. Friction has been particularly serious in India. Much of this has been inspired by Hindu fanatics, whose greatest "success" was in 1969 in the Indian industrial city of Ahmedabad, north of Bombay, where about 4,000 people, mostly Muslims, were slaughtered. But this was only the most extreme example: communal clashes, often serious, constantly occur.

These have been a factor second only to Kashmir in Pakistan's maintenance of a powerful standing army. Secular India's failure to maintain its own secular standards or, as Pakistanis see it, India's persecution of its Muslim minority, has helped to speed the anti-India bandwagon in Pakistan, particularly in West Pakistan, which does not need a healthy economic relationship with India so much as does East Pakistan. The treatment of India's Muslims, especially as magnified by the considerable distortions of the Pakistan government's propaganda machine, has consistently reinformed notions of a "jihad," or holy war, against India and has, thereby, buttressed the case for maintaining a strong and sizable army. Pakistan's army of about 300,000 men is 62 percent larger than India's in proportion to their respective populations and nearly three-quarters of Pakistan's budget now goes on military spending.

There were, further, the defense problems created by the shape of Pakistan on the map. The two "wings" of Pakistan have been, in themselves, a major defense handicap, creating severe logistic problems—1,000 miles apart by air but, as far as bulk supplies and heavy equipment are concerned, 3,000 miles and a good week's journey apart by sea. Pakistan also inherited nearly all the border problems of Britain's former Indian empire, notably along the northwest

frontier. And there were, in addition, 3,000 miles of new
frontiers—the lines of Partition on a map, of no geographical
significance and therefore not, like mountains or rivers, readily
defensible. East Pakistan is almost entirely surrounded by
India; and the most vital area of West Pakistan, running from
Karachi northwards through Lahore toward Rawalpindi and
Peshawar, includes the great trunk road of West Pakistan and
its main rail links—jugular veins within easy striking distance
of the Indian border.

All these military considerations made a strong army essential for Pakistan. But the army also came to have a decisive
political role. For Pakistan's political development suffered
two massive blows very soon after Partition. Only a year after
the new nation was born, Mr. Jinnah, its "father," the "Quaid-i-
Azam," died. Then, three years later, the assassination of his
right-hand man and first prime minister of Pakistan, Liaquat
Ali Khan, left Pakistan bereft of political leaders of stature.
With a man of Jinnah's strength and authority at the helm,
Pakistan could perhaps have been steered through the shoals
of early nationhood to a stable maturity. As it was, its political
life degenerated rapidly into a squalid tangle of corruption and
self-seeking. Tensions, basically economic but needing sound
political solutions, built up between the two wings and between the provincial units within the West wing itself. Wrangling and delay in the legislature over the framing of a constitution declined into a game of political intrigue. By 1958 the
nation's affairs had reached a state of chaos, and despite a
boost to the economy generated by the Korean war, Pakistan
was approaching bankruptcy. In October the generals decided
they had had enough. Under the lead of the commander-in-
chief, General Ayub Khan, they effected a bloodless *coup
d'état,* dismissed all the politicians, dissolved the legislatures,
abrogated an unsatisfactory constitution devised over the
course of eight years, and imposed martial law. It was the
beginning of an eleven-year rule by Ayub Khan which
molded Pakistan into the military dictatorship which it remains to this day.

It was, as events were to prove, unfortunate that the army
should have come to political power in Pakistan. But it was at

least understandable, even reasonable. For it was the army, at the time of Partition, which alone kept its head while all around crumbled, which alone upheld law and order amidst the chaos which swept across the land. In the flux, this efficient, trained, above all disciplined, military machine, an institution carefully created and groomed by the British, alone held firm. When the nation, under the politicians, again came near to foundering, it seemed the only proper course to most Pakistanis that the army should step in and get a grip on the country once and for all.

Ayub Khan's coup marked the end of what had passed for parliamentary democracy in Pakistan. Although the outward forms of the country's political structure subsequently changed from time to time, they did so always at the behest of the generals. It was the army which henceforth ran Pakistan; it was army rule which fired the spirit of revolt among a mass of unrepresented and underprivileged people; and it was under the army that Pakistan descended into its present desperate crisis.

UNBENEVOLENT DICTATORSHIP

Democracy cannot work in a hot climate.—
PRESIDENT AYUB KHAN

The years of Ayub Khan's presidency were Pakistan's heyday. The takeover by the top corps of Sandhurst-trained officers was engineered with great intelligence, with no bloodshed and the very minimum of disruption. The new regime stamped down on corruption in government and business, rigorously weeding out venal civil servants and sending the discredited politicians into deserved obscurity. The highly able hard core of the civil service was able to get on with the task of administering the country without the incubus of incompetent and self-interested ministers. The threads of the economy were firmly pulled together again. Tens of thousands of urban refugees who had been living in appalling squalor ever since partition were resettled with impressive speed and vigor. One of the worst of the many pullulating shanty colonies which disfigured the towns was on the road from Karachi airport to the city center, giving Pakistan a deplorable image in the eyes of almost all visiting foreigners: it was quickly bulldozed away under military direction and 500,000 people in Karachi were rehoused in satellite townships. President Ayub's brisk new government also tackled Pakistan's backward agriculture, where still feudal tenurial systems impeded the development of improved techniques and made it necessary to continue the expensive import of food from abroad. The purge of corrupt politicians and officials was followed by moves aimed at stripping excess landholdings from feudal landlords. The reforms, even though they never worked out to the extent intended and largely failed to curb the political power of the landed aristocracy, were nevertheless an index of the new government's zeal and intentions and, with its other moves, confirmed the view of many in Pakistan that the army knew how to get things done and had its priorities right. Side by side with this, Pakistan's international stature was steadily enhanced and President Ayub flowered, if briefly, into a statesman of international significance.

With notable boldness, Ayub confronted the basic problem of Pakistan's inability to evolve a democratic system suited to its particular needs and difficulties. Parliamentary democracy had patently failed: at any rate, Pakistan's politicians had patently failed democracy. And, to the army's leadership, it was equally patent nonsense to expect a largely illiterate population to be able to grasp complex political issues sufficiently to participate in a Western-style parliamentary process: they took a classically elitist view. This led Ayub to formulate his electoral system of "basic democracies." The entire country was broken up into thousands of tiny constituencies, containing only about 1,000 people, and voters elected representatives from each of these areas. Representatives from each group of ten constituencies formed a "union council" and this indirect elective system proceeded upwards tier by tier, with nominated members being added to councils at each ascending stage, up to the national assembly itself, which was chosen by an electoral college distilled from the basic democratic process. Under a constitution promulgated in 1962, the President retained considerable executive powers. By these means it proved possible, later that year, to lift martial law.

And yet, it all went wrong and came to naught. Why?

It was, first, that bane of Pakistan's sad history, the problem of Kashmir, which started the rot. Over the years, it had proved as intractable as ever. The Indian attitude hardened with steps to bring the part of Kashmir that it held into the Indian union as a constituent state, in apparent defiance of undertaking given earlier. In 1965, after a series of incidents along the cease-fire line, full-scale war broke out. It lasted three weeks before petering out under the weight of heavy losses. Although Pakistan was not seriously worsted in the encounter, the war, concluded in an aura of spurious good will with a treaty signed under Russian auspices at Tashkent, was the death knell of the reign of Ayub Khan.

At the outbreak of fighting, the government imposed a series of emergency regulations, including indefinite detention without trial. Many of these were not rescinded when fighting stopped. Three years later, hundreds still languished, untried, in the jails. The regime had become increasingly harsh in its treatment not merely of critics but even of basically sympathetic (and certainly patriotic) critics. The war also aroused deep disquiet in East Pakistan. For the Kashmir issue meant very little to the Bengalis—they neither felt involved in it, or concerned about it, nor felt they had anything to gain from Kashmir's accession, if it could be achieved, to Pakistan. Yet East Pakistan had, willy-nilly, become involved in the war. It had been a heavy contributor toward the costs, though it could ill afford it. And, even more crucially, the war against India had left the east wing cut off from the west and undefended for seventeen days by anything more than one army division. The feeling that East Pakistan's security had been jeopardized for the sake of West Pakistan acutely vexed Bengali sentiment. It seriously intensified anti-West wing opinion already hardening in East Pakistan, for a complex of reasons which are discussed in the next chapter.

But it was not only the Kashmir war and its consequences that brought Ayub down. For those realities of military dictatorship lying hidden behind the façade which Pakistan's leaders skillfully presented to the world—and, for a time, to their own people—eventually came, in all their ugliness, to the surface. From 1962 the government, ostensibly civilian, in fact continued as a catspaw of the military circles surrounding Ayub—a reality symbolized by the removal of the national capital from commercial Karachi to Rawalpindi, the seat of the army's general headquarters. And this reality was not merely a military government, but a dictatorial one at that. There was never the freedom of expression enjoyed in most Western democracies or, more pointedly, in neighboring India.

Military rule might have seemed fine at first—efficient, disciplined, incorrupt, honorable, purposive. But the actuality was otherwise. Ayub Khan's constructive, reformist, even progressive social policies, aimed at giving a modern shape to this still new nation, eventually turned sour because they gave the semblance of political freedom without its substance. Bitter experience taught that the system of "basic democracy" did not work: the elected representatives were too easily cowed or corrupted by the regime. Land reforms were circumvented by the landlords. Corruption was stamped down but not stamped out: in the last years of Ayub's presidency, it was more rampant than ever, pervading the civil service, commerce, business, even the army, even the president's own family—and on a blatant scale. The government's only answer to increasing restiveness was increasing repression. By late 1968 this had built up a head of steam which blew the lid off the pressure cooker and overthrew what had by then become a hated, feared regime.

This parlous situation was well described by Air Marshal Asghar Khan, former chief of the Pakistan air force, a widely respected, courageous and selfless figure. In November 1968 he announced his entry into politics as an opponent of Ayub. "Graft nepotism, corruption, and administrative incompetence are affecting the lives and happiness of millions. Social inequality and economic disparity are increasing. Telephones are tapped, opinion is shackled, the Opposition is shadowed and jailed, no one can express his views fully."

The students were the first to revolt. They had become increasingly restive under curbs on their political activity, including laws which went so far as to provide for the forfeiture of degrees by graduates deemed to be "subversive." In November 1968 they launched an agitation for educational reform. This developed into widespread rioting after police killed a student at a demonstration. A young man came near to assassinating President Ayub at Peshawar, which was followed by the internment of Ayub's former foreign minister, the mercurial Mr. Bhutto, on charges of inciting the students. The rioting spread, and took on a more general political character. Within days it broke out also in East Pakistan. Although Ayub now backtracked rapidly in a bid to save his position, it was too late. Faced with growing disorder, he offered in February 1969 to negotiate with Opposition leaders over their program for thoroughgoing constitutional and economic reform. He ordered the release of Mr. Bhutto and other political prisoners, including the East Pakistan leader, Sheikh Mujibur Rahman, facing trial on a trumped-up conspiracy charge. Ayub further announced that he would not seek a further term of office. But it was no use. The masses of Pakistan's disparate wings had found common cause and were making sweeping demands: direct elections and full democracy, ending of press censorship and similar curbs, abrogation of the emergency regulations, wide-scale nationalization, and, above all, a large measure of autonomy for the East wing. And this was the "crunch." For although Ayub conceded two fundamental demands, for parliamentary government and direct elections, he stalled on the others. A massive wave of strikes in West Pakistan, which brought immense disorder, was magnified in the East wing, where unrest spilled over into violence and the breakdown of authority. On March 24, 1969, President Ayub resigned. Martial law was reimposed. The army's commander-in-chief, General Yahya Khan, took over the reins.

Pakistan survived that crisis of 1969. But despite the efforts made since, the nation degenerated into an even graver crisis only two years later, into the crisis which is the civil war and human disaster now being enacted. And this is because the basic errors which led to Ayub's downfall were not corrected and, indeed, in many cases could not be corrected. For Pakistan is based on fundamentally fallacious premises which are, of their very nature, beyond correction, and which produce a social, economic, and political infrastructure which is irremediably flawed. Army rule had soon turned stultifying and repressive under Ayub; but, despite all of Yahya Khan's good intentions, the same happened under him—except, as if proving a point in psychopathic psychology, it happened more quickly and more cruelly. The attempt to get parliamentary democracy to work failed before the advent of Ayub, who gallantly tried to find a way of making it work; the attempt has likewise foundered under Yahya Khan, who has also sought a way to make it work. The immense and largely justified sense of grievance in East Pakistan which burgeoned under Ayub, as its economic inferiority to the West wing and the many other discriminations it suffered became more glaring, only marginally diminished under Yahya Khan. The government of Yahya Khan has been unable to find a way of reconciling East wing needs with West wing demands, of making one nation out of what are essentially two. Yahya's new broom wore out just as quickly as Ayub's: corruption, for example, was weeded out but has again proliferated. Yahya has failed just as Ayub failed. Both men failed because the faults they were seeking to correct, or at least ameliorate, were too big and too basic, far beyond solution by patchwork reforms, formulae, or compromises. The lessons of the rise and fall of Ayub have been paralleled exactly during the leadership of Yahya Khan, which began in March 1969. What happened under Ayub happened again under Yahya, only more so, because a one-nation Pakistan is, fundamentally, a fallacious concept.

And it is East Pakistan which is the crux of the problem.

5

SIX POINTS

Does the mouth, belly, and stomach of East Pakistan lie in West Pakistan?—SHEIKH MUJIBUR RAHMAN

East Pakistan is today the world's most serious long-term problem area. The civil war that has savaged its land and people in the spring and summer of 1971 and the even greater holocausts that threaten to engulf it, are a direct result of its chronic neglect and cynical exploitation since Partition by Pakistan's predominately West wing leadership.

East Pakistan is luckless in its geography, history, sociology, politics, economics, and culture. Some of this we have already seen in Chapter 2. Historically, its troubles date from as far back as the thirteenth century, when invading Muslims converted masses of lower-caste Hindus in East Bengal to their faith. It was that conversion which led, seven centuries later, to East Bengal becoming, for no other reason than that its people happened to be almost all Muslim, an artificial, half-national entity known as East Pakistan. So little was it really regarded by Pakistan's founders that Jinnah, for example, declared in a speech at Dacca in 1948 that Pakistan would have only one national language, and that would be Urdu. At that time, 55 million Pakistanis spoke Bengali and only 6 million of West Pakistan's people spoke Urdu. Jinnah was howled down by his Bengali audience, scores of whom were imprisoned for such *lèse-majesté*. There, in a nutshell, were the seeds of the conflict that has ravaged Pakistan.

But for centuries after the Muslim conversion and conquest, East Bengal remained prosperous, with its fertile soils, fish-laden rivers, world-coveted spices, its jute and the muslins of the now long-dead mills of Dacca. It was this very prosperity which attracted the East India Company to East Bengal, and it was under the unbenevolent rule of British merchant adventurers that the region descended into the penury which has afflicted it ever since.

As East Pakistan began, in 1947, so it has remained: the poor relation, used and exploited by the West wing. But by March 1969 its problems had become insupportable. The province was seething with discontent and clamoring for its fair share of the national cake—or, at any rate, the national crust.

The problems of East Pakistan by this time had become so immense that it could truly be described—even more so today —as a permanent international disaster area. A senior Western diplomat stationed until recently in Dacca used to compare the region to Lake Erie, where gross neglect has caused such intense pollution that the lake has become virtually dead. Like Lake Erie, East Pakistan could only be saved by an international rescue operation of massive scale and cost. That, of course, has not been forthcoming.

It is, first, an area of great and repeated natural disaster. At least a quarter, sometimes half, is flooded in a typical monsoon season. A death toll of hundreds drowned annually is normal. Intense poverty, virulent disease such as smallpox, typhoid, and cholera, massive illiteracy, enormous unemployment, are only some of the problems that plague East Pakistan.

Basic to them all is the demon problem of overpopulation. At Partition, East Pakistan's population was around 40 million. By 1961, it was 51 million. By the time of Ayub's overthrow, eight years later, it was 18 million more. Today it stands at about 75 million and is rising at such a rate, nearly three million a year, or 250,000 a month—a rate which will itself inevitably increase—that in five years' time, even if there are massive death tolls from war, famine, and calamity, it will be of the order of 90 million. By the end of the century—

that is, in a generation's time—it could well be 250 million.
Today, nearly half (47 percent) of its population are children
under fourteen. And this is an area half the size of Britain. And,
too, these are figures which assume implementation of effective
birth control schemes—which are not being implemented in
practice.

Because of the intense population pressure and the conse-
quent pressure on land, East Pakistan has for years been
unable to grow enough food to feed its own people. The basic
diet is rice. Paddy is grown on such a scale that there is no
more cultivable land to be had, without reducing the equally
vital jute crop. Even so, 1.5 million tons of food has to be
imported each year. But because communications are poor,
distribution is inefficient and inequitable, food costs are high,
black markets and rackets of every kind proliferate, and
thousands of people, especially children, annually suffer and
die from chronic malnutrition.

The typical family income in East Pakistan is less than a
rupee (twenty-two cents) a day. Unemployment is so acute that
for every advertised vacancy there are 2,000 applicants—or,
at least, were, until the brute might of the army this spring
and summer sent thousands fleeing from Dacca and every
other town, leaving these places all but deserted, so that their
economies, already failing, collapsed. The wisest, and luckiest,
man I knew in East Pakistan was the professional worker
(who earned more and lived far better than most Bengalis)
who told me in 1969: "I'm getting out. What is the point of
going on living here? My future only gets worse. For my children, it's hopeless." For a year after that he watched his future
get worse. Then, just in time, he escaped.

It is the poorest and most overcrowded area in the world.
The thousands killed annually by cyclone, flood, disease, and
hunger go unnoticed. Yet, East Pakistan's problems have been
consistently ignored, overlooked, and belittled by Pakistan's
leaders—always in deed and usually in word too. Their
purblind disregard produced the upsurge of 1969. It was that
continuing explosion of revolt which by 1971 proved impossible to contain any longer without resort to extreme force.

East Pakistan is the majority wing, with about 55 percent

of Pakistan's total population, and it has consistently earned two-thirds of Pakistan's foreign exchange with its exports of jute and tea. Nevertheless, it has annually received less than a third of the nation's imports, less than half of its development funds, and less than a quarter of its foreign aid. Its *per capita* income is only two-thirds of that in the West wing. The West wing, with a smaller population, has nearly four times as many hospital beds, and has had three times as many new polytechnic institutes. Until General Yahya Khan became president, Bengalis were sedulously kept out of almost all key posts in the central civil service at Islamabad, in the diplomatic service, and in the judiciary. In the army, all the senior officers and nine out of ten other ranks have come from the West wing: this has meant that East Pakistan's people have received only a fraction of the 1,500 million rupees ($326 million) paid to the soldiers each year, money which would have been tantamount to an agricultural subsidy, as much of it would have been saved and sent home.

The economic imbalance between the two regions was in part, as we have seen, an inheritance from the British. After the unchecked depredations of the East India Company in the days of Clive and Hastings, it was consistently treated as the Cinderella area of the subcontinent. As we saw in Chapter 2, Partition was particularly hard on East Pakistan, depriving it totally of the jute mills which were the sole outlet for its one cash crop and only substantial revenue earner. East Pakistan was also cut off from its natural market in West Bengal and its natural port, Calcutta. In the years after Partition, successive administrations made only the feeblest efforts to put all this right.

During the 1950s and '60s, jute mills were built which, by 1970, were able to process about a quarter of East Pakistan's output: better than nothing but still not much, not enough. Some effort and money went into developing Chittagong as a substitute for Calcutta, but this was inevitably insufficient for the region's needs, and road and rail links with Chittagong, way down the "panhandle" of East Pakistan, are still inadequate. A few, relatively small water-control and irrigation projects had been undertaken, but far short of the extent needed. For although it is a region of heavy rains and giant rivers, East Pakistan vitally needs not less but more water, controlled irrigation—particularly as the vast and inexorably growing population makes it increasingly essential to grow more than one rice crop a year. But the work begun was minimal. The largest project in the province, at Kobadak on the Ganges, far from complete, was put at a cost of 509 million rupees ($110 million), woefully short of the sums needed for even the most basic flood and irrigation works.

And woefully behind, also, the sums spent in West Pakistan. More than ten times as much was devoted to the giant Mangla and Tarbela dams—built at much greater speed—in West Pakistan. The new capital at Islamabad aptly symbolized the grotesque disparity between the two wings. This handsome but extravagant new city, which should never have been the priority it was for a developing nation, in itself had cost 527 million rupees ($105 million) by 1966, and was still far from complete. Already more had gone on this *folie de grandeur* than on the one major flood-control and irrigation project in East Pakistan, where hundreds, sometimes thousands—and in 1969 500,000—drowned annually and hundreds of thousands were permanently semistarved. Although later a "second capital" was begun at Dacca, as a sop to Bengali sentiment, it too proved aptly symbolic; never finished and of a weird design seemingly full of giant holes, like an Emmenthal cheese. It seemed to sum up the parlous state of East Pakistan.

The deliberate policy of creating a "have" West wing and a "have-not" East wing was self-interested to the point of callousness and, as events have proved, monumentally shortsighted. But it would be unfair to ignore here the impulses that were valid and the conditions that were given which also underlay that policy.

For it was the West wing, where the drive and know-how were, that was the making of Pakistan. The Bengalis tended to do only what they were best at: talking. Almost inevitably, Pakistan's capital had to be in the West wing, either at Karachi, its mercantile hub, or Rawalpindi, the army's headquarters. The location of the capital, as London and Paris show, can crucially affect a nation's entire economic balance, or create an imbalance such as that illustrated by the north-west-southeast disparities in Britain. The concentration of political and administrative power acts like a magnet on economic interest and "decentralization" is ineffective. Moreover, from the start, Pakistan's strongest vested interests were in the West wing: the major entrepreneurs who had emigrated from Bombay, India's commercial metropolis, to Karachi; the powerful landlords of Sind and Punjab; the influential Islamic mullahs, or priests; and, of course, the Punjabi-dominated army. And industrial development also went ahead in West Pakistan because, from the very beginning, its infrastructure was superior—communications, for example. The rudimentary industry with which Pakistan began was almost entirely in the West and was mainly in textiles, and was therefore the natural springboard for development alongside the main cash crop of the West wing, cotton. In the East, by contrast, there was no industrial base, no coal, oil or minerals, and, because of the flat terrain, no exploitable sources of hydroelectric power. The East, in fact, was desperately handicapped, an extremely difficult base on which to build. The lion's share of development effort, therefore, went to the West wing largely because there were far better prospects there of earlier and better dividends. And defense requirements also made it important to build up the strength of the West wing first.

But, of course, this situation was avidly exploited. The East wing soon became a colony, or at least a captive market. It was exploited in two main ways. On the one hand there was the negative exploitation, whereby it was starved of development funds and economically throttled to the advantage of the West wing. On the other it was positively exploited by being made the dumping ground for the West's low-grade but costly textiles and other manufactures. Because Pakistan was cut off by political considerations from trade with India on any scale, these could be sold nowhere else, and East Pakistan was unable to buy from anywhere else. The rapacity which made the fortunes of the most enterprising, aggressive, or corrupt West wing industrialists and entrepreneurs, the famous twenty-two millionaire families, was inexcusable. These families, the Adamjees (jute and textiles), the Saigols and Valikas (textiles and chemicals), the Haroons (*Dawn* newspaper and car assemblies), the Habibs, Hyesons, Fancys, Dawoods, and others, owned two-thirds of the nation's entire industrial assets and four-fifths of its banking and insurance.

In the end, there could be only one result. The chronic disparities between the two wings, the crushing burdens which poverty in all its aspects heaped upon the Bengalis, and the stifling of political expression under Ayub, proved intolerable. They combined to produce the eruption of passions in East Pakistan which, in blood and turmoil, propelled Ayub Khan from office into the obscurity of his walled villa in Islamabad. And having been ignited, those passions continued to blaze. To this day, though repeatedly suppressed, they have not been extinguished.

The East wing's situation was summed up by President Ayub himself. In a broadcast a month before his enforced resignation, the President admitted: "People want direct elections on the basis of adult franchise. I realize also that the intelligentsia feels left out. People in East Pakistan feel that in the present system they are not equal partners, and also that they do not have full control over the affairs of their province."

Exactly. What was admitted by President Ayub Khan then, and has not been in any way corrected, despite attempts, is today vehemently denied by Pakistan's official spokesmen and unofficial apologists. But even President Ayub himself had had to admit the facts.

It was this situation which inspired the "Six-Point Formula" for regional autonomy of the strongest East wing party, the Awami ("People's") League. This program, expounded by its leader, Sheikh Mujibur Rahman, remained the basis of East Pakistan's demands all through the martial-law period of President Yahya Khan until the outbreak of civil war in March 1971 made it obsolete.

The Six Points demanded:

1. The establishment of a federal form of government, with a parliament, to be the supreme point of power, directly elected by universal adult suffrage.

2. The federal government would control only defense and

foreign policy, leaving all other subjects to the federating states of East and West Pakistan.

3. The two wings would have separate (but freely convertible) currencies or, if one currency, separate fiscal policies to prevent the flight of capital from East to West Pakistan.

4. The federal government would have no powers of taxation. It would share in state taxes for the needs of foreign and defense affairs.

5. Each of the federating states would have the power to enter into trade agreements with foreign countries. They would also have full control over their earned foreign exchange.

6. The states would have their own militias or paramilitary forces.

The Six-Point Formula, subtitled in its pamphlet form "Our Right to Live," was supposed to be the basis for the solution of East Pakistan's problems. The demands were put forward repeatedly and forcefully by Sheikh Mujibur Rahman both in speeches to his people at mass rallies and in rounds of abortive political negotiations which preceded Ayub's departure. Sheikh Mujib came to national prominence during the so-called Agartala conspiracy trial in 1968, when, with thirty-four other defendants, he denied charges of conspiring with Indian agents to plot an armed revolt against West Pakistan. The trial, a blatant political frame-up, collapsed ignominiously during the last days of Ayub's presidency. But it was the making of Sheikh Mujib.

Although styled "Sheikh," Mujib came from a comparatively humble village background. He was born in March 1919. At Islamia College in Calcutta, he was a poor student, and failed several exams, but, showing the capacity for "management" which later made him the Awami League's leader, he "managed" to graduate. It was at Dacca University's law school, soon after Partition, that he rose to stature as a political leader, and was expelled after tough and tireless work on the students' behalf. In 1949 he helped to found the Awami League, Pakistan's first Opposition party, and was soon in jail, branded as a "communist" and "disruptionist." He was to spend ten of the next twenty years in prison, but in his periods of freedom used his superb organizing ability to marshal the

Awami League into a powerful political force. Tall and well-built, with a thick mustache and features rather like Stalin's, Mujib is a family man and an inveterate pipe-smoker. When still a small boy, he was betrothed in a marriage arranged by his parents, in the traditional way, to his three-year-old orphan cousin. His wife, Begum Mujibur Rahman, who bore him three daughters and two sons, herself became a key figure in the inner circles of the Awami League and a strong political influence not only on Mujib but on other party leaders.

Mujib was always a compelling public speaker, particularly in Bengali. His crowd speeches, more in the nature of eight-eenth-century orations, never failed to fire and enthuse the Bengalis. But despite this, and despite Mujib's penchant for lurid imagery, and his somewhat fierce public demeanor, he was essentially a moderate, even conservative, leader. Others in East Pakistan, notably the octogenarian Maoist leader Maulana Bashani (who, in 1946, "discovered" Mujib and groomed him for leadership), favored more drastic courses. Mujib, however, told the Agartala conspiracy court that he did not believe in unconstitutional methods, that while he favored regional autonomy for East Pakistan he did not favor secession. Every aspect of Mujib's policies and actions in the period since then substantiate those claims, despite his being publicly labeled, and libeled, a "traitor" by Yahya Khan.

But it was the tragedy of Mujibur Rahman and of East Pakistan's millions that their legitimate and minimum demands, embodied in the Six Points, invited not moderate, but extreme consequences. Indeed, extreme consequences were a corollary of the Six Points. It was this which caused the constitutional deadlock which followed the 1970 general election and which, in turn, led to civil war.

For the Six-Point program envisaged a system in which there was a federal government that controlled only defense and foreign policy, and would therefore be unworkably feeble; a federation in which the two wings had not merely separate currencies but separate economies, a prescription for chaos; a system which allowed the East wing its sorely needed trade agreement or at least some trading arrangements with India, in contradiction to a federal policy which, because of Kashmir, would continue to be hawkishly anti-Indian. Furthermore, it was a system which would totally undermine the status of the army, making it rely for its subventions on an economically independent East wing. Such a proposed system hit at the very foundations of Pakistan as it existed. It might call for mere autonomy, and not spell out secession, but secession would be its effect. And why should the West wing ever accept? It had so much to lose and so little to retain from any agreement to the Six Points.

Yet the paradox was this: while the Six-Point Formula went far beyond what West Pakistan could conceivably grant, it was the least that East Pakistan could demand. The formula, in short, succinctly implied the fundamental irreconcilability of the two wings of Pakistan. It was not the Six Points that made the 1971 armed conflict between the two wings inevitable: it was because that conflict was inevitable, because their interests inevitably conflicted, that the Six Points were produced.

The massive East Pakistan demand for the Six Points ousted Ayub and brought General Yahya Khan into the presidency. This was the opening scene in the denouement which rent Pakistan and quenched Muhammad Ali Jinnah's dream of a nation dedicated, above the ruck of mere factional concerns, to Islam.

6

BACK FROM THE BRINK

The armed forces must save Pakistan from disintegration.—PRESIDENT AYUB KHAN

The situation in East Pakistan when General Yahya Khan came to power on March 25, 1969, was appalling. Mob rule and jungle law prevailed. The social fabric had collapsed. All recognized authority had broken down or abdicated its responsibilities. The students of Dacca University, Pakistan's largest, controlled the city, though "terrorized" was more usually the case than "controlled." The basic democrats, some of whom were murdered, were replaced by "People's Councils" whose elections were "organized"—gerrymandered, that is— by the students. Political unrest was accompanied by repeated strikes, some general, and the widespread use of "gheraos," in which strikers locked managers inside their offices until they met the workers' demands. Some jute workers wanted 150 percent wage increases. The police refused to intervene in hundreds of vicious disputes in factories, offices, schools, and government departments. Even doctors and nurses went on strike.

In the villages, the situation was worse. As the "basic democracy" system collapsed, local government evaporated. Peasants went on the rampage settling old scores, particularly against the many "basic democrats" who had been local landlords and moneylenders, and also against such other symbols of Ayub's authority as the police, rent collectors, and non-

Bengalis. "People's Courts" gave a blank license for massacre. Hundreds were found "guilty" of "antipeople crimes" and were burnt alive, beheaded, crucified, knifed, drowned, or hacked to death. As the wave of anarchy swept across the province, the economy was shattered. Food stores were looted and rice distribution to needy areas impaired or blocked completely. Food prices soared as a result, far beyond the ability of the average man to pay. A flight of capital from the region began which, unchecked in the next two years, was to bleed East Pakistan white. As the rich scrambled to convert their rupees into "hard" foreign money, the black market exchange rate rose to treble the official level. It was a truly revolutionary situation.

Significantly, it was not the government that took the first steps to restore order, but the students and the Awami League under the leadership of Sheikh Mujibur Rahman. The man who is now publicly accused of treason by President Yahya was in fact the man who took the initiative which helped to save Pakistan from the abyss in March 1969. Far from encouraging the secessionists, anarchists, student hotheads, and other extremists, Sheikh Mujib publicly urged the government to reassert itself and take action against the forces of disruption. The Maoist peasant leader, Maulana Bashani, was calling on the peasantry to turn the province into "another Vietnam." Mujib, essentially a moderate, saw this for the folly it was and had sufficient leadership qualities of courage, vision, and authority to save the situation.

Ayub, however, proved unable to assert authority. General Yahya Khan, a close friend of Ayub's, took over as Chief Martial Law Administrator. Soon afterwards he became President.

Agha Muhammad was then fifty-two. He had had a fine military career, serving with the old Indian army during the Second World War in North Africa, in Iraq, and in Italy, where he was taken prisoner and escaped, a remarkable achievement in the circumstances. He had been commander-in-chief for three years. General Yahya had never taken part in political life. His entire training as a soldier was opposed to any such involvement, and everything in his character and background confirmed the sincerity of his expressed distaste for the political role thrust on him. Yahya Khan was a soldier's soldier, and he looked it: short but solid, clipped accent, unsmiling, strutting and always wielding a short silver-topped swagger stick. He was regimental in bearing and demeanor, regimental in attitude, a man whose relaxations were those of a typical soldier: heavy drinking in the mess and gallivanting outside it. He made little secret of these tastes and interests.

Bluffly but characteristically, in his first broadcast to the nation, in his customary tongue, English, General Yahya disclaimed any political ambition. His prime duty, he declared, was "to save the nation from utter destruction"—it was his duty as a soldier. Establishing martial law, he laid down a series of the harshest punishments for strikes or creating disorder, undermining or even criticizing government authority, or holding unlicensed public meetings; there were a range of lesser penalties, including whipping and forfeiture of property, for other infringements. These were necessary, the president said, because normal law-enforcing methods had broken down. "The armed forces could not remain idle spectators to this state of near anarchy. My sole aim in imposing martial law is to protect the lives, liberty, and property of the people and put the administration back on the rails. I have no ambition other than the creation of [these] conditions." General Yahya then averred his faith in the process of transferring power to the freely elected representatives of the people. He gave his assurance that the army had no political ambition. It simply aimed to provide a "sound, clean and honest" basis for an eventual return to civilian government.

General Yahya's forceful but patently sincere appeal struck home. Disorder evaporated, almost without incident, without the army having recourse to force. Strikers returned to work on the day of his broadcast. The schools and universities reopened at once. And the new regime gave solid evidence of its good will. Students' fees for the next five months were waived by government decree. Many workers were granted wage raises of up to 50 percent. Stockpiles of grain and sugar were sent to East Pakistan. By the end of March, the armed troops who had been put to guard the key points in the cities were back in barracks. The crisis which nearly brought Pakistan crashing had, by a masterly exercise of firm and fair government, been dispelled.

The image of good intention was reinforced by a second speech after the general became president, on March 31. Again disclaiming political ambitions, he explained that he had had to become head of state only to fulfill administrative and diplomatic obligations until a new constitution was framed. Fresh measures, which for the first time in years gave millions of Pakistanis hope for the future of their nation, followed day by day. In contrast to the imposition of martial law in 1958, political parties were not abolished, although their activities were severely restricted. The new president, however, said they would be allowed to campaign again as soon as "present passions" had cooled. And he made his policy as clear and explicit as could be. He told a press conference: "Our aim must be to establish constructive political life in the country so that power is transferred to the elected representatives of the people." But this could be done only on the basis of a discipline that enabled the elections to be fair and free. The administrative structure, which needed "cleaning up," had been damaged and could not be put right overnight. He would take wide-ranging advice about the composition of a new parliament and the form of elections. And as for East Pakistan's demands for autonomy, he said: "It is entirely for the elected representatives of the people to decide what they want." This was a view to which President Yahya consistently adhered, despite many opportunities and possible excuses to modify or even retract it, through to the general election of December 1970 and beyond, through the constitutional crisis which followed—almost to the eve of unleashing the army's might to deny the people of East Pakistan what they had "decided they wanted."

But of this there was no evident clue, even until the very end of the 1971 constitutional crisis. President Yahya gave repeated signs of his democratic intent. As Ayub had done, he stamped down on nepotism and corruption in the civil service and elsewhere, but with more effect. He quickly launched into a series of talks with leaders of the many parties

which made the Pakistan political scene so confusing and
flew to Dacca for four days of discussions with Sheikh Mujib
and others. Then he returned for discussions with Mr. Bhutto,
the youngest and most forceful of the politicians, almost the
only one on the scene with future potential as a national leader.
Once again, in defiance of protocol and precedence, the president paid a four-day visit to Dacca to see Sheikh Mujib. And
this was more than mere window dressing. On July 28, 1969,
only four months after taking power, President Yahya appointed a chief election commissioner, promised elections
within eighteen months, and appointed a civilian cabinet of
ten which included, unprecedentedly, five Bengalis. He told
the nation: "The banning of political parties and political
activity would not be in the interest of the country. It would
make the task of administration a little simpler but would
delay the achievement of our goal, the transfer of power to
the elected representatives of the people. It is my declared
intention to usher in a sound and robust democratic system."

In a frank, open way, he outlined some of the political
problems the nation faced. There were, first, too many political parties, and he urged those of like views to merge, reducing the unmanageable number. This was wise advice. For the
double disaster of Jinnah's early death and Liaquat Ali Khan's
assassination had left Pakistan with politicians who had never
been able to rise out of the ruck of self-seeking intrigue and
bickering, concerned not with nation but with faction. Such
men and their parties were rightly seen as a menace to the
return of constitutional government. This soldier-president, no
politician, was no less able on that account to give a basic
lesson in politics not only to Pakistan's bemused people, but to
the politicians themselves: "Before we can arrive at an ac-
ceptable solution, we must abstain from parochial and sub-
jective considerations." The politicians must either rise above
this, he stated, or there might be no election at all and the
president himself would have to impose a new constitution
from above.

Secondly, the president said, there were deep problems over
the basis for the new election and the new parliament. Some—
East wingers—wanted voting on the basis of population

(which, of course, would give East Pakistan a built-in majority in the national assembly). Others—from the West wing— wanted the two wings to have equal representation. It was highly significant that the president should go so far to acknowledge and publicize the demands of the East wing, but he went even further, and wrung a good measure of confidence from the still disaffected, sullen, and rebellious masses of East Pakistan by declaring: "One of the reasons for dissatisfaction in the East wing was a feeling that they were not being allowed to play their full part in the decision-making process at the national level and in certain important spheres of national activity. In my view, they were fully justified in being dissatisfied with this state of affairs."

How disastrously ironic those frank words were to seem in the spring and summer of 1971, as Bengal writhed and wept under the military heel.

But again, this was in the uncharted future, discernible only by pessimists with political radar. In 1969 it was one measure of President Yahya Khan's success that he was able to dispel pessimism by inspiring a nationwide trust in his authority and integrity. Even in East Pakistan, where there had at first been grave suspicion about his motives and intentions, doubt was allayed. And the impressive army-led cleanup continued. There was a massive purge of corrupt civil servants: 303 senior officers were suspended for peculation and maladministration. An inquiry began into the police. Increased minimum wages were fixed for industrial workers. The right to strike was soon restored. There were sweeping educational reforms which gave staff and students greater participation in the running of universities and Bengali and Urdu were made official languages in *both* wings of the country. For a martial law regime, all this was notably constructive and liberal-minded. Such actions underlined the relatively *un*-martial approach of the regime, which so successfully gave it the stamp of an unimpeachably selfless cadre, dedicated to the people rather than to vested interests, as alive to the needs of the under-privileged East wing as to the demands of West Pakistan. It was of a pattern with the setting-up, in the regime's earliest days, of a complaints center where popular grievances could be attended to. Also, later that year President Yahya pardoned a number of students in Dacca who had broken martial law regulations by staging a political demonstration. To some at the time, this seemed like "weakness." The students had actually gone into hiding and challenged the president to a direct confrontation by threatening to strike if arrest orders against student leaders were not rescinded. But by sidestepping this, dismissing the students as "young and emotional boys" who had acted through "ignorance or overexuberance," the president displayed not weakness, but political agility and strength. It took the sting from the situation and the wind from the sails of extreme leftist elements, overrepresented among the students, who, as the president rightly observed, "actually wanted chaos" as a prelude to a peasants' or workers' revolution.

The process of preparing an election continued smoothly, for the time being, and without interruption. In August 1969, President Yahya ordered the preparation of electoral lists on the basis of universal adult franchise. These were to be published in June 1970, by which time 60 million voters would be enrolled. Then, on November 28, came President Yahya's most important announcement. The general election would be held on the following October 5. The voters would choose a constituent assembly, whose members would have 120 days —no more—to frame a constitution. If this failed, the assembly would stand dissolved and there would be new elections. Unrestricted political activity would be allowed again in the new year. And the President set three basic goals. First, voting would be on the one-man (and one-woman), one-vote principle, for the first time in Pakistan's history. This would give East Pakistan, with 55 percent of the nation's total population, a permanent and assured majority of votes, and would end the earlier voting parity between the two wings. Secondly, in response to popular demand from local interests in West Pakistan (and as a counterweight to the first undertaking), West Pakistan would cease to be one administrative unit, on a par with East Pakistan, but would be broken up instead into four provinces, *each* of equal status with East Pakistan, the country's fifth province. And thirdly, the two wings would have "maximum autonomy." But—and this was to prove the crucial proviso in the months to come—that autonomy must be, would have to be, consistent with the integrity and solidarity of the nation. The "fully justifiable" dissatisfaction of the Bengalis at being left out of making vital national decisions must be set right, President Yahya said. However—and here again the words were to seem bitterly ironic—he could see "no reason" why it should not be possible to work out a satisfactory relationship between the central government and the provinces, giving the regions, notably East Pakistan, control over their own resources and development without affecting overriding national interests controlled at the center. There was, alas, every reason, as millions of Bengalis were to find to their cost.

But the announcements, at that time, augured well. So well, for example, that Air Marshal Asghar Khan retired from political life, stating that his object in entering politics had been achieved with President Yahya's announcement of an election. On March 28, 1970, to mark the first anniversary of his coming to power, the President gave the nation the long-awaited details of his "legal framework order," the blueprint for a return to civilian government and the creation of a parliamentary democracy. The new national assembly would have 300 elected seats (plus 13 reserved for women). Of these, East Pakistan, on the basis of its population, would have 162 compared with the West's 138. Here, at last, was the ultimate acknowledgment of East Pakistan's supremacy in the union, the admission of the principle that it was entitled not merely to an equal say, but to the greater say, in how the nation should be run. It was a breakthrough and the acid test of the sincerity of the regime's democratic intentions. Or so it seemed.

The legal framework order stipulated that the new constitution must be Islamic, that Pakistan must remain a federal unity, giving as much provincial autonomy as possible but retaining a strong central government, and that it must make statutory provision for removing the economic disparity between the two wings. The legal framework order set the seal on President Yahya's master plan for the peaceful transfer of power to a democratically chosen civilian government. He had made it repeatedly plain, in public and in private, that his one wish was to return to soldiering and his one commitment was to democracy. To those he still remained true. The way now seemed clear for the emergence of Pakistan, after much travail, as a full-fledged democracy.

7

FLOOD AND FAITH

*Pakistan, unfortunately, is not a flowing river: it has
to be only a lagoon by the very circumstances of its
creation.*—NIRAD C. CHAUDHURI

But the way to democracy was not to be so smooth. The
monsoon, which annually brings both fertility and death to
East Pakistan, saturated Bengal that August even more
thoroughly than usual. The rains inundated millions of acres,
drowned at least 100 people and uncounted hundreds of live-
stock, destroyed 95,000 homes, submerged at least 250,000
of the miserable shacks and shanties that so many Bengalis
regard as "home," brought the usual wave of epidemic disease,
damaged crops worth about $190 million over an area of
15,000 square miles and, by wrecking roads, bridges and
culverts, virtually turned most of an area the size of England
and Wales into a vast, unmanageable, unadministrable swamp.

At the best of times, East Pakistan is a depressed, depres-
sing, run-down and neglected area. In a normal monsoon,
crisscrossed by a myriad of swollen streams and overflowing
rivers, it becomes difficult to run as even a quarter-efficient
unit. But the monsoon of August 1970 was exceptionally
heavy. It created such chaos that every civil servant, including
all those assigned to the complex job of operating the election,
was put to the task of bringing relief and order. The president
flew to Dacca and toured the region. After days of detailed

consultation, he decided to postpone the election for two months. It was the first serious setback to his well-phased program.

It was a courageous decision, for it clearly exposed him to the suspicion that he did, after all, want to prolong military rule and his own hold on supreme power, and had snatched the first opportunity. The facts, however, belied this. For one, the President gave a new date, December 7, for the poll. It would have been just as easy not to do so. Also, the new date was well chosen: far off enough to enable the East wing to pull itself together, not so long delayed that winter snows would make polling difficult in the hill regions of West Pakistan. President Yahya's sincere determination to hand over power stood this test. There can be no question that he was both sincere and accurate when he said that "the alleviation of human misery" must be the nation's first task. This was generally accepted as a valid reason for postponing the poll. Anyway, many of the political parties welcomed the extra two months as a period of grace in which to salvage their declining prospects. Quite above this, it would have been impossible to organize a genuine election in such hopelessly disorganized conditions, affecting nearly half of East Pakistan's 162 constituencies. And if the election had been held as scheduled, polling would certainly have been so low that the results would have had little worth or meaning.

President Yahya's postponement, therefore, was an honorable and sensible decision. How strange it was to seem, then, when far greater disaster struck, that "the alleviation of human misery" was not given proper priority. The election postponement had extraordinary consequences, as we shall see. But to have foreseen them then would have been impossible—except to the Almighty Allah himself.

And such a comment is not frivolous, as it perhaps appears.

For the story of Pakistan in those last fateful months of 1970 was almost as if Allah had willed the course of events, an Allah whose concern was to block and wreck the transition to parliamentary democracy.

For Allah, in the sense of the ethos which prevails in Muslim communities, is transparently no lover of democracy. At any rate, the art or knack of running a democratic system has consistently eluded every predominantly Muslim nation from Algeria in the West to Indonesia in the East. The leading Muslim nations of the Middle East (or, as the Asians understandably call it, West Asia), countries like Egypt and Saudi Arabia, are bastions of dictatorship and monarchy, and every other Muslim state is an oligarchy of one kind or another. Pakistan, whatever the superficial appearances might have been from time to time in its short and checkered history, was never an exception.

Given that Pakistan is, above all else, a Muslim state, it is hard to see that it can ever escape from this straitjacket. For the Muslim is imbued with a consciousness of his religion to a far deeper extent than the everyday Christian. Islam, like Hinduism, imposes a pattern on society and life which cuts right through transient political moods, forms, phases, or ideals. And the essence of Islam, its stress on an Allah who does not just exercise, like the Christians' God, omniscience and omnipotence (mere abstract concepts) but is also paternalistic in the much more concrete matters of everyday life, helping the Believer even in his meanest bazaar transaction— this essence of Islam, far removed from the Christian idea of free will, is fundamentally antidemocratic. For it demeans, in fact it denies, the role of the simple individual in shaping society, in however humble a way. It encourages and facilitates a political buck-passing from bottom to top. Almost inevitably, it throws up an Allah-substitute—a Hussein, Sukarno, Nasser, or Ayub—as a surrogate father figure and leader on whom the masses feel they can depend. This is very much how it was with Pakistan, from Jinnah (named Quaid-i-Azam, or Great Leader, and frequently referred to as Father of the Nation), to Ayub and Yahya, and it is no accident that in just the same way Sheikh Mujibur Rahman became the darling of the Bengalis.

Pakistan also suffered a further handicap: it was politically part of the Indian subcontinent. Even a brief look at the charade of India's politics during the previous few years was a discouraging prospect for India's offspring and nearest neighbor. Parliamentary democracy in New Delhi was foundering in a sterile morass of politicking and rubber stampism. The corruption of state politics and the open contempt for the democratic process displayed by Mrs. Gandhi, India's prime minister, where she saw fit, were poor auguries and poorer examples for Pakistan. The failure of Indian politics was yet a further sign of how difficult it would ever be to induce democracy to take root and flourish in Pakistan, where almost everything, from subcontinental mores to geography, to the climate, to the national and religious ethos, seemed stacked against it.

The omnipotent Allah, it would seem, took due note and so decreed that before the election of December 7 a new disaster, one that dwarfed even the August monsoon in magnitude, should strike the wretched people of East Pakistan.

THE CYCLONE

. . . the heavy and the weary weight of all this unintelligible world.—WORDSWORTH

The cyclone disaster of Thursday night, November 12–13, 1970, was the greatest natural disaster in modern times. In six swift hours something like 500,000 people were sucked and swept away into the deeps of the Bay of Bengal or washed up, battered to pulp, along the serpentine shores of the Ganges estuary. If the total was more than 500,000 dead, no one can deny, for the catastrophe totally outstripped human ability to make any reliable reckoning, and unofficial local estimates put the death toll at well over 1,000,000. But these were "guesstimates." The unreliability of any cyclone statistics must begin with the fact that no one knew, or ever will know, how many men, women, and children were living in the stricken delta region at that particular time. The fact, however, that the official death total, 207,000, accounts only for corpses actually recovered and certified as dead by responsible officials, is indication enough that this was a disaster of almost incomprehensible extent. It had the profoundest effects in the months to come on the future and shape of Pakistan.

The cyclone developed far out in the Bay of Bengal five days before it hit the East Pakistan coast. It was first spotted by American weather satellites. Weather stations around the world received warnings that it was moving northwest and was of severe intensity, with winds of up to 100 miles an hour. So much is not uncommon in that part of the world. But on Tuesday, November 10, it suddenly altered course from northwest to northeast and headed direct for the Ganges delta area of East Pakistan, in the constricted northeast corner of the Bay of Bengal. When the storm reached the coastal belt and off-shore islands, winds of up to 150 miles an hour were being generated. The tempest hit at midnight and was not spent until dawn. From the Sunderbans in the West to Chittagong in the East, along 300 miles of coastline, there was almost total devastation.

Only the sturdiest structures in the hardest-hit part of the region, the few "pukkah-built" brick houses, could withstand such forces. The ramshackle lean-to's, bamboo huts, and other feeble dwellings of the typical Bengali stood no chance. Even so, thousands of people might have been saved had they had adequate warning. But there were no adequate warnings, no cyclone shelters in this area where cyclones came repeatedly, and no means either of protection or escape for many thousands of people. Such failings were a telling commentary on the neglected condition of East Pakistan. Furthermore, it quickly transpired that there were no emergency contingency plans, almost no provision for assessing damage and providing relief, and no awareness among the West Pakistan leadership, until spurred by the wave of shock that went round the world, that this was a massive human disaster.

To be fair, it must be said that this cyclone was unprecedentedly severe. Any relief organization would have been overwhelmed by it. But because of chronic neglect of even its most pressing problems, East Pakistan was not prepared for the onslaught of any cyclone at all, or for the aftermath. And this was, of course, a failing of governments more concerned with serving the vested interests of West Pakistan than the needs of the East wing. This was how the cyclone, as its full horror unfolded and the full inadequacy of government relief measures became clear, turned into the most vivid possible demonstration, at least in Bengali eyes, of the way in which Pakistan's predominant West wing had failed its eastern partner. Not the disaster itself but the massiveness of its effect was the direct consequence of distorted and self-interested political and economic policies.

The failings of the West wing were shown in scores of ways. The weather authorities, for example, knew the cyclone was approaching and duly put out a warning. But few of the 2,000,000 or perhaps 4,000,000 people in the delta region ever received it, for few had the radios to pick it up or could be told by those who did. Many thousands of people had come to the delta at that time for a few weeks of harvesting and were living on up to 200 islands whose only communication with the outside world was by boat. Thousands more lived in similar isolation permanently. It might seem absurd to argue that this was the fault of West Pakistan, but the fact that so many people were living, or had come to harvest, in a notoriously dangerous area, regularly hit by cyclones which annually claimed hundreds or even thousands of lives, was in itself an index of East Pakistan's chronic problems of overpopulation and land hunger. It would never have been within Pakistan's resources to have solved these problems, but that they existed to the extent they did, and still do, was a direct outcome of officially sponsored, planned, and condoned neglect of the entire area.

Likewise, although many of the most heavily populated islands of the Ganges delta were nothing more than glorified sandbars, no more than twenty feet above sea level at any point, there were no high concrete platforms to which people might retreat, let alone sufficient sea walls. Here again, it would be unfair to minimize how huge and costly such works would have been, had they been undertaken. Thousands of platforms would have been needed and thousands of miles of sea wall up to twenty-five feet or more high, and this in a land without almost any stone, and the cost has been estimated at more than $100 million by World Bank experts. But the fact is that there was just nothing on which thousands of people in the area could depend for their lives if a cyclone came except good luck, the ability to climb a tree which might withstand the storm and to which they might manage to cling, or the fortunate chance of being near enough to a strong "pukkah-built" house to take shelter.

These sins of omission by the Pakistan authorities—dominated by West Pakistan interests and constrained always by West Pakistan economic priorities—seemed, indeed, heinous enough. But they were of the past, and President Yahya had created a sufficient impression of sincerity and good will to remove much Bengali resentment. But to these sins the authorities now crassly added indifference and ineptitude on a massive scale.

The cyclone hit on Thursday night and by Sunday it was already clear that it had hit uncommonly hard. Unofficial but reliable death counts were already approaching 100,000 and dozens of islands still remained unvisited. Yet even by the following Tuesday, the government was still somnolent. The chief anxiety of relief officials—and precious few of them there were —seemed to be to play down the scale of the disaster and the number of dead. Clearly, they faced a rescue operation that was completely beyond them. But their attempts to minimize the disaster inevitably discouraged and delayed the provision of food, medical, and other relief supplies from abroad.

It seemed incredible, but there it was—in this land where cyclones, of greater or lesser intensity, are part of the way of life, where floods and storms kill, maim, and render homeless thousands of people every year, the man in charge of rescue and relief work was a part-time official. The much harassed Mr. Anisuzzaman, not surprisingly, was out of his depth, with no contingency plans worthy of the name, no coordinating committees, no control room to organize the relief effort at even the simplest level (so that some jobs were done twice and others not at all), no communications with great stretches of the affected area.

The government did not declare East Pakistan a disaster area. It did not give the situation the official status of a national emergency. Such steps would have given the relief commissioner authority to spend money on the scale needed and, further, would have diverted the entire national effort into the relief operation. Instead, it was all left to part-time officials, volunteers, and foreigners. Only a few companies of the large West Pakistan army stationed in and around Dacca were called out to assist, and desperately needed boats and vehicles belong-

ing to various government departments continued to be used
for normal purposes, or even lay idle.

Five days after the twenty-five-foot-high tidal wave, borne in
by the cyclone, had submerged the delta region, I visited one of
the worst-hit islands, Manpura. This and other densely populated islands in the Mouths of the Ganges had taken the brunt
of the storm. The fields were littered with human corpses and
animal carcasses, now stiff, purpling, and bloated. "We have
buried hundreds. We haven't the strength to bury any more," a
village councilor said. The air now was still and empty even of
vultures—even they had been swept away. It was a scene of
horror. On Bhola, a larger island to the west of Manpura, at
least 50,000 people had been drowned; on Hatia, eastward,
there had been at least 80,000 fatalities. But all this horror
seemed outweighed by the fact that then, five full days after
the disaster, the first outsiders to visit the island were foreign
journalists. It was typical of the way Pakistan officialdom had
failed to measure up to its responsibilities.

In the days that followed, those failings multiplied, and as
the failings multiplied the silence of Islamabad became more
eloquent and the indifference of the nation's West Pakistani
leaders to the sufferings of the East wing became more evident. This was their meanest hour.

9

HARVEST OF NEGLECT

I wish to God something had been done ten years ago.—PRESIDENT YAHYA KHAN

A month earlier, commenting on the August flooding, in a statement on the Bengali service of the BBC, President Yahya Khan had promised to appoint a cabinet minister who would be "solely responsible" for dealing with floods in East Pakistan. But he failed to honor that promise. It seemed a token of West Pakistan's indifference to the problems of the East wing. In March, it is true, he had announced a multiproject flood-control and water-resources scheme, and by the time the cyclone hit, World Bank experts were in the area working on preliminary plans. But the government showed no sense of urgency about the project—though it was urgent—and there was no indication at all how it would be paid for except a vague allusion from the president to "a suitable contribution" from his government.

The situation in Dacca was extraordinary. The administration was paralyzed. Officials as hapless as the cyclone victims themselves gaped open-mouthed at press conferences and left it to foreign journalists to put forward suggestion after suggestion for improving—or, more accurately, for initiating—the relief effort. Vice-Admiral S. M. Ahsan, East Pakistan's governor, a humane and thoughtful man, seemed as woefully afflicted with paralysis as his minions. As resentment rapidly

mounted throughout the province over the patent failure of the
West wing to take any substantial action over the disaster,
and as the official death toll continued to mount, and as
desperately needed supplies, arriving now from abroad, also
mounted up at Dacca because the authorities had made no
provision for distributing them, Admiral Ahsan confessed at a
press conference that he did not even know the answers to
some of the most pertinent questions. He did not know, for
example, why only one of Pakistan's many military helicopters
was available for the relief effort, or why so few soldiers were
being used.

Again, it was symptomatic of the total gap, not only in
geography but ultimately in fellow feeling, between Pakistan's
two wings.

And for all the sincerity of President Yahya Khan he could
not rise above his own limitations. He remained what he was
—the soldier from West Pakistan (although not quite the
"simple soldier" as he liked to see himself), who viscerally felt
and at times could not conceal his dislike and contempt for the
Bengali majority of this so-called nation. That 1,000-mile gap
was simply too much, even for the president: the difference
and distance between Punjabis and Bengalis was irreducibly
as great as between Scots and Turks, or Bretons and Kurds,
or Cubans and Lapps.

President Yahya erred appallingly in his handling of the
cyclone disaster. When it happened, he was in Peking, con-
cluding a successful four-day official visit. Fresh from, and
flushed by, this triumph, the president took off for home. On
the plane he duly celebrated, and when the plane landed at
Dacca, diverted because of the cyclone news, the president
was clearly none the better for his flight. He quickly made an
aerial tour of the disaster area, which he later claimed had
been a thorough survey of the scene. This, in fact, was nonsense. It was a rush job, made not by helicopter (as claimed)
but by plane, which flew much too fast and, at 3,000 feet,
much too high for the president to be able to discern anything.
Back at the airport, before returning swiftly from sweaty
Dacca to sweeter Islamabad, the president uttered a few ritual
expressions of sorrow but was heard quite plainly to mutter:

"It didn't look so bad." It was another ten days before he returned to East Pakistan, but by then it was too late to eradicate the image of callous West-wing indifference to and even disdain of East Pakistan's tragedy. To Bengalis, the president's aloofness appeared in marked contrast to the way in which dozens of foreign countries contributed readily and speedily with manpower, materials, and money.

What brought President Yahya back to Dacca was not chiefly a desire to galvanize the lethargic Pakistani relief effort (though this was a welcome and overdue by-product) but to retrieve his own sorely damaged "credibility" and to confront a new storm—the surging tidal wave of Bengali resentment. This now threatened to engulf the nation in a major political crisis. Indeed, it posed a direct challenge to the regime. Pressure was mounting for a second election postponement, but that was trifling compared with the pressure wave of disgust directed at the government, the West wing's relationship with the East wing and therefore the very basis of the nation itself. Newspapers of the East wing, despite rigorous penalties prescribed for criticism of the martial law authorities, were bitterly scathing. They waxed in repeated denunciations of the leadership. The Dacca Sunday newspaper *Holiday* was only one among several. It hit out at what it called "total petrification of the central government." President Yahya had failed to meet his obligation to the country. "We know we don't have the right to question this. Yet we dare it for once. Our people can bear it no more. The regime has failed the East wing."

The mass mood reflected that judgment. Antigovernment demonstrations were growing daily more frequent and more angry.

Sheikh Mujibur Rahman, of course, caught the mood. For two weeks he was silent, touring the disaster area and working with survivors to help them pull the threads of their lives together again. But, as it began to look as if President Yahya would be forced to postpone polling yet again, Mujib voiced his first strong challenge to the martial-law regime. It was, indeed, an ultimatum, delivered from a position of strength, in front of television cameras from around the world.

There would be civil war if the election was again postponed, he warned. East Pakistan would break away from the union. "East Pakistan will owe it to the million who have died to make the sacrifice of another million, if need be, so that we can live as a free people." These were to prove tragically prophetic words.

If it had been unaware before, the martial-law leadership way in Islamabad would certainly have known now the ugliness of the mood in East Pakistan. Mujib charged them with "criminal neglect." Had he the power, he would bring those responsible to trial: "They are guilty of almost cold-blooded murder. They deserve the most severe punishment. Our rulers have been tardy, callous. The textile millionaires have not given a yard of cloth for our shrouds. They have a huge army, but it is left to British marines to bury our dead." (This was a reference to the British task force which had come to the Bay of Bengal from Singapore to help with relief work.)

President Yahya gamely sought to restore confidence in his administration. He did a superb public relations job at an international press conference held in the governor's palace at Dacca on November 27. He candidly admitted that mistakes had been made: "My government is not a government of angels. Nothing is ideal. Our efforts have not been ideal. But we have done our damnedest. They were the best, the most that could be done." And to critics like Mujib who taunted him with being absent from Dacca, the president was curt and cutting. It was his job, he said, to organize and supervise, and the best place to do that was the seat of government. His advice to Mujib, if he did not like the way things were being run, was to come into power as soon as possible—"the sooner the better." But if Mujib ran the country as he was advising Yahya to do it, "nothing would happen."

This performance showed the president to be the consummate politician that he claimed not to be. His answers went a long way toward disarming his foreign critics and, by announcing that the election would be held as planned, on December 7, except in eight or nine cyclone-hit constituencies, he defused the political crisis. But the damage had been done nonetheless. The Bengali masses knew what Mujib had told them in Bengali; they knew little and cared less what a "foreign" president lectured to them in English. They gave their verdict just over a week later, giving Mujib the most sweeping election victory ever won outside a one-party state.

In the months to come November's cyclone had the profoundest effects on the future and shape, indeed the very existence, of Pakistan. Seldom can a natural event have had such far-reaching political consequences.

To the Bengalis of East Pakistan, the cyclone was ultimate proof—if proof they sought—of the perfidy of their West Pakistani overlords and administrators and what Sheikh Mujib called "coteries"—the 22 millionaire families, the landlords, the army.

The government could not, of course, he held responsible for the cyclone itself, as President Yahya felt obliged to plead. But the toll of dead and destitute, homeless and bereft was quite another matter. For it had been a statistical certainty that such a cyclone would hit East Pakistan, if not in 1970, then sooner or later, probably sooner. There had been disastrous floods in August. A hurricane in October, which hit the Ganges delta, went virtually unreported though it killed 300 people. There were major cyclones in 1960, 1963, and 1965. Such things were commonplace. The area itself was tailor-made for catastrophe: low-lying, unprotectable except at vast expense far beyond Pakistan's resources, subject to flooding from the sea, from some of the heaviest monsoon rains in the world, and from the Ganges and Brahmaputra river systems which carry a volume of water equivalent to nine Mississippis. Not much could be done about all this without a major international effort—but that required a Pakistan initiative which never came, until too late. Given the rising population, a new, immense disaster was inescapable and inevitable, yet when it finally struck, the relief administration was so enfeebled and neglected that it was not even up to the task of counting the dead.

So the cyclone also brought with it political disaster because many of its effects demonstrably arose from years of neglect: failure to provide shelters, failure to provide an effective warning system, failure to initiate projects, failure to bring enough aid at enough speed, failure to respond in a human way to a human tragedy, and the ultimate failure of all, the failure in kinship, as the Bengalis saw it, by their fellow Muslims of the West wing. The upshot was the smashing victory for Sheikh Mujib and the Awami League at the polls.

Pakistan's deep sickness was demonstrated by the way in which the cupidity, venality, and blatant opportunism of a variety of personal and vested interests came in the wake of the cyclone. The fact that 500,000 people perished and 2,000,-000 were made homeless was forgotten with a speed or exploited with a relish that even the case-hardened cynics of the 150-man international press and television corps in East Pakistan found shocking.

In the stricken area itself, corrupt local officials were soon demanding a fee of two rupees (more than a day's wages for many people) before they would distribute relief supplies. Police successfully compelled the government to pay them ten rupees, well over normal rates, for burying corpses.

At the time of the August flooding, local officials and politicians had often exaggerated the extent of the damage, bad though it was, in order to get more money and other aid from the central coffers. This probably accounted in part for the government's initial indifference to the November cyclone. "Those Bengalis again," was a common attitude. Nevertheless, despite its enormity, the tragedy was cynically exploited for political purposes. In places, Awami League supporters got preference over others with greater need for relief supplies. Distribution of relief was used as an election bribe. The situation was, of course, a handy stick to beat West Pakistan with: some saw it in no other light. Bengali nationalists were quick to spread alarmist rumors and to exaggerate the already appalling death figures in order to raise tension and resentment against West Pakistan and, incidentally, divert attention from Bengali corruption and bungling.

Thousands of beggars who normally scraped out a sustenance-living in the streets of Dacca moved into the disaster area to obtain relief supplies meant for others. Such was the measure and depth of East Pakistan's degradation.

But the world shared in it, too. For it quickly became clear that the sudden rush by Western nations to contribute emergency aid was as much a matter of "one-upmanship" and prestige as simple charity. After all, this was an area they had relatively ignored or neglected, in spite of the best advice, for years.

The United States Ambassador, Mr. Joseph S. Farland, turned the American effort into an egregious personal public-relations exercise in which he was frequently photographed by the U.S. Information Services in various absurd and contrived glad-handing situations. The Americans sent thousands of cans of food, but no can openers—a clear example of an exercise conceived in terms of public relations rather than victims' needs. Other nations, anxious to keep up with the international Joneses, sent fur coats, boxes of unmarked pills (water-purifying?, medicinal?, contraceptive?) and food which needed cooking for areas where there was nothing left to cook with.

The British High Commissioner, Sir Cyril Pickard, confided that his own country's notably generous and effective contributions had been made "counterproductive" because of criticisms of the Pakistan government in the British press. Britain sent a combined-services task force equipped with helicopters and landing craft. It brought 3,000 tons of relief supplies into the Petuakhali area, and doctors vaccinated thousands against cholera and smallpox. It was an admirable piece of work. But although the task force was described by its commander-in-chief as "tailor-made" for such a job, the task force did not sail for well over a week after the cyclone. It did not sail, in fact, until somebody in Whitehall suddenly woke up to the fact that the cyclone was not so much a dreadful disaster about which something should be done, as a "tailor-made" opportunity for justifying the new British government's policy of maintaining a task force in the Far East. So the Defense Ministry public-relations office went into full swing: Britain sent more public-relations men to Pakistan than doctors.

Even the Catholic Church got mileage out of the disaster. On his way to Manila on November 28, Pope Paul made a technically unnecessary touchdown at Dacca so that he could hand over a check for $10,000 to President Yahya. The money did not, of course, have to be delivered personally. But with the world's press and television conveniently present, though on other business, the publicity for the Vatican was cheap at the price.

It's an ill cyclone that blows nobody any good.

10

PEOPLE'S VERDICT

The status quo *is not for purchase.*—Z. A. BHUTTO

So now Pakistan was not only handicapped by physical division and stunted political development, but also ravaged by a collapse of confidence by the majority wing, by the anguish of natural catastrophe, by mounting economic burdens, by rising social pressures, and by a stability made precarious because of the extreme uncertainty of its future. At this crucial time, December 1970, Pakistan faced its greatest political test.

The auguries for democracy were depressingly poor. Despite presidential advice, the politicians had proved unable to raise their sights to any notion of a national polity. It was significant that the man who now seemed most likely to become prime minister if a civilian government were formed, Sheikh Mujibur Rahman, remained solely concerned with securing autonomy for East Pakistan. He hardly thought in national terms. Sheikh Mujib made a fine Bengali orator and was a born political leader. But he was lacking in any basic political philosophy and hadn't even the haziest ideas of how he would conduct a government. The leadership of the other parties seemed similarly inadequate. The parties themselves remained almost as numerous as ever, despite some polarization on the Left and Right, which was more a reflection of their continuing concern for petty position than their concern for political principle. There was no sign, beyond sloganeering, that anyone had worked out a coherent platform or policy for the future.

Despite his notable forbearance toward these deficiencies, an ominous sign of regimental impatience began to show through President Yahya's avuncular declarations. In his March 1970 broadcast he came to a point near both anger and despair: "I regret to say I have noticed a rather unfortunate tendency on the part of some of our leaders, first to urge the administration to be firm whenever violence breaks out in any particular area and then, once the lawbreakers are arrested and the legal processes of justice begin, to shout themselves hoarse in demanding the release of the very people against whom they so vociferously demanded action. It is obvious this is done with an eye to the gallery. We cannot afford . . . to act in a shortsighted manner merely to obtain some sort of tactical gains in the political field."

The prospects for the successful making of a constitution seemed dim, very dim. It had, after all, taken eight years to draw up the previous one, and that had quickly proved unsatisfactory. The new assembly would have only 120 days. Despite the provision for it to be dissolved if it failed, and for a new election in that event, it seemed unlikely that this could in fact happen. For the nation was by now politically satiated. The election campaign had lasted, in effect, well over a year; the political parties were financially as well as otherwise exhausted. Yet, the task of making a new constitution for Pakistan was enormous in its complexity. By some almost magic formula, the assembly would have to find the right balance between national unity and the powerfully conflicting pulls of the two opposite wings, and between federal power and provincial autonomy. At the same time, it would have to satisfy the demands of the four new provinces which now made up West Pakistan, each demanding its full share of the cake on a par with Pakistan's fifth province, East Pakistan. Yet it would also have to recognize East Pakistan's preponderance, but do this without letting it dominate the nation. Furthermore, it was impossible to see how the Punjabis, the key element in the making of Pakistan, the most energetic and enterprising of its peoples, could ever acquiesce in a whittling away of their dominance, either by the Bengalis of the East or by their now nominally equal neighbors in Sind, Baluchistan, and the North-West Frontier province. And even this was not all. For the Legal Framework Order had laid down that the new constitution must be true to the tenets of Islam. But that same constitution could not ignore the growingly powerful attitudes, secularist and pragmatic, of the young and educated. In any case, no one, least of all the religious factions, could agree what the tenets of Islam were. Many of those who regarded themselves as the true inheritors of the Prophet saw "Socialism"—not the thoroughgoing kind involving wholesale nationalization in which Mr. Bhutto purported to believe but merely any measure of social reform—as anti-Islamic heresy. Khan Abdul Wali Khan, leader of a left-wing splinter group called the National Awami Party, shrewdly observed that the terms "Islamic" and "Muslim" were almost impossible to define. Any attempts to do so would quickly be exploited by antidemocratic elements. And certainly deep dissension existed over the "minimum qualification" for being a Muslim, and large sectarian minorities such as the Shias (to which the president himself belonged), the Ismailis, and the Ahmadiyas, who wanted a constitution based on the strictest interpretation of Islamic credo. It was hard to see how any constitutional formula could subsume such a welter of conflicting interests and attitudes. And even if it were possible to devise one in theory, by means, for example, of a bicameral system which safeguarded minority concerns in its upper house, or a presidential system with strong executive and overruling powers vested in the head of state, on the de Gaulle model, such "solutions" could never really affect the issues in practice at the grass roots level, where the social and political antagonisms would remain.

You did not have to be a pessimist to be skeptical in the extreme about the prospects for a return to democracy in Pakistan, let alone the creation of a stable parliamentary system. President Yahya had already recited the failings of the politicians. He saw them as they were: a menace to the re-institution of civilian government. The 120 days allotted to the constituent assembly, even allowing for preliminary talks to iron out procedural problems and settle the parameters of debate, would scarcely suffice for devising such a masterpiece of compromise. And even if, by some miracle, it succeeded, what then? For how could the Awami League, pledged to securing maximum autonomy for its people, ever find common cause with the disparate groupings of the other wing, at least for long enough to form a stable government? No conceivable coalition could work. But neither could any conceivable government dominated by one—any one—factional party. President Yahya may have been a reluctant recruit to government, but he was not the man to shirk his duty as he saw it. He would never hand back power if the likely result would be a return to chaos. He had already acknowledged, in private, that he might have to continue as head of state. Pakistan had been put on the road to democracy only by this strong man at the wheel. The need for strong leadership in a large developing nation rent by schism was being thoroughly demonstrated in neighboring India, where parliamentiry democracy was well established. How much more it seemed, therefore, that Pakistan would continue to want and need the same strong man at its head, election or not.

But when it came, the election seemed to sweep away all misgivings. Despite fears of incidents and intimidation, voting went peacefully, with polling stations and other key points well guarded by soldiers and armed police. There was no question that the poll was both fair and free. Voting had not been expected to be heavy, but it was, and women, going to the polls in Pakistan for the first time, turned out in large numbers. The conduct of the poll was itself a tribute to the efficiency of its preparation, under President Yahya Khan's leadership, and to the innate good sense of the mass of the people in ensuring that it passed so smoothly. Then, as the results came out on a warm December night from Radio Pakistan in Karachi, it soon grew clear that, for all the confusion and complexities, and indeed for all the novelty of the process in which they had participated, the 40 million who voted out of the 56 million on the rolls had, though largely illiterate, understood the basic issues. They voted in a coherent way, as the situation, if not the politicians, demanded of them. In East Pakistan,

they voted almost to a man for Sheikh Mujib. The Awami
League won 151 out of the 153 seats contested (and on
January 17 won all of the nine cyclone-affected constituencies
where voting had been postponed). Thus, at a stroke, the
Awami League had not only the majority of the new assembly's
East wing seats, but an absolute majority over all other parties
combined. In the West wing, the result was almost as decisive.
Mr. Bhutto's fledgling People's Party, with hardly any party
machine and dependent almost solely on the charisma of its
leader, took 81 of the 138 seats. Only these two parties, both
moderate, despite their slogans, both socialist, won substantial
support. The welter of other parties, all associated with the
Ayub and pre-Ayub period, received a drubbing. The voters
could hardly have made it more clear that they overwhelmingly
rejected the old order, overwhelmingly wanted a new start under new leaders for Pakistan. Six of the old major parties,
which each fielded more than 100 candidates, were almost
wiped out. They won a total of only 30 seats, not one of them,
of course, in East Pakistan. Among the vanquished parties
were the various Muslim Leagues and the Jamaat-i-Islam
group, voices of the most powerful and orthodox religious
interests, whose appeal was now humiliatingly spurned by the
voters. Ten days later, elections to provincial assemblies only
confirmed the general election results. It did indeed seem, for a
brief spell, like the dawn of a new era, and President Yahya
Khan was quick to acknowledge Sheikh Mujibur Rahman as
"next prime minister of Pakistan."

But the result was, in a tragic, paradoxical way, too good,
too clear-cut. For it created not merely a two-party assembly
but a two-nation assembly: it emphasized the separateness of
the two wings. Mr. Bhutto's People's party fought not a single
contest in East Pakistan, while the Awami League fought only
a token handful, seven, in the West wing, and lost them all.
The two wings, separately represented, were thus polarized.
Though the two parties had much in common on the surface,
with their vague socialistic nostrums of nationalization and
land reform, these were no more than slogans, with little
prospect of ever being put into effect. But they did differ on
two fundamental points: Mr. Bhutto's deep-rooted opposition

to maximum autonomy for East Pakistan—his insistence, that is, on a strong central government—and secondly, his demand for a tough stand against India (a 1,000-year war, as he put it) over Kashmir, which was anathema to Sheikh Mujib. Here, right away, were the first obstacles to a coalition, fundamental differences of approach on both the constitutional and political planes.

It was hard, even, to imagine the two men working well together. Zulfikar Ali Bhutto, then forty-two, had trained as a barrister and entered Ayub's cabinet when only thirty years old. At the age of thirty-four he was foreign minister, a post he retained until breaking with Ayub over the Tashkent agreement. Brilliant, sophisticated, world-traveled, and born to wealth, Bhutto is as witty and silver-tongued in private as on the public platform. Beside him, the humbler, less-polished Mujib, in his ill-cut waistcoat, seemed, for all his power as a crowd orator, a comparative rustic, and Mujib certainly felt this. In their rare meetings, the two men had failed to "click." And their differences went deeper, too, for Mujib was moved by profound, if narrow, principles, whereas it is doubtful if Bhutto has ever been actuated by any political principle greater than his own overweening hunger for power.

Yet, if the assembly was to work at all, there had to be a coalition, a meeting of minds, an accommodation, between these two. For no possible grouping could outweigh the Awami League, leaving it out in the cold, and the Awami League, despite its absolute majority, could not conceivably be allowed to go ahead on its own, or without the support, even if only tacit, of Mr. Bhutto.

It was now time for the postelection talks which President Yahya, in his prepoll broadcast, had suggested. No date for the assembly meeting, when the 120-day countdown would begin, had yet been fixed. The President considered that this was the time for the political leaders to "arrive at a consensus on the main provisions of our future constitution. This will call for a spirit of give and take, trust in each other, and realization of the extreme importance of this particular juncture in our history."

Even if there had been a spirit of give and take (of which

there was little), or of trust in each other (of which there was none), the president's call for a consensus was a pipedream. The leaders were opposed on the very fundamentals.

All this soon became chillingly clear. So far from giving or taking, Sheikh Mujib insisted on the unconditional acceptance of his Six Points. He would accept no compromise on that, he declared. He also unconciliatingly refused to budge from Dacca and come to West Pakistan, if only as a gesture of "trust," for talks with Mr. Bhutto. In response, Bhutto, with greater tact, said he would do all he could to help frame a constitution, and was willing to make compromises "here and there." But there could be no compromise on the unity, solidity, and integrity of Pakistan—all of which, of course, were fundamentally affected by the Six Points.

The dispute escalated. By December 22, only three weeks after the election, Mr. Tajuddin Ahmed, the Awami League's secretary and later to become first "prime minister" of a seceding East Pakistan, declared that his party, having won an absolute majority in the national assembly in what no one disputed was a fair and free election, therefore had a clear mandate and was "quite competent" to frame a constitution and form a central government on its own.

Such a statement was typical of the dreamland in which so many Pakistanis, and above all Awami Leaguers, continued to dwell. It simply was not a matter of practical politics to think of the Awami League, however large its majority, running the country and framing the constitution on its own. The East wing, it is true, had been governed by the West for a generation. The reverse would be utterly unacceptable, even if workable. Later, when the West Pakistan army went about insuring the integrity of their nation by bayoneting children and slitting women's throats, even intelligent Pakistanis in the West wing managed to persuade themselves that most Bengalis really wanted the army to wrest control from the Awami League.

Mr. Bhutto's attitude crystallized accordingly. He told a press conference a week later that in a federation there must be a consensus of all the federating units, that is all five provinces, if any future constitution were to last. Forming a government, he tactfully admitted, was one thing, and one-party government might be possible. But constitution-making was another matter. And now came the first threat, the first sign of incipient conflict: "If the Awami League insists on making a constitution to its own liking, we will step aside. And the People's Party will not be responsible for the consequences."

The battle lines were hardening. Sheikh Mujib again showed himself to be the moderating influence in his party, leading from behind, by declaring on January 3, 1971, that his party would not frame a constitution on its own, even though it had the majority. But it still proved impossible to find common ground. By now it must have dawned on President Yahya, for the time quietly isolated from the political process he had set in motion, that his scheme was going to fail. It doubtless seemed, as perhaps he had feared in his March 1970 broadcast, when he warned the politicians about playing to the gallery, that they simply were not up to governing the country. And the president knew what he would have to do.

11

POLITICIAN'S JUDGMENT

So are they all, all honorable men.—SHAKESPEARE

Early in 1971, it gradually grew more difficult to book seats on the daily Pakistan International Airways flights from Karachi to Dacca. Like any good soldier, or head of state, President Yahya was putting his contingency plan, long ready, into operation. Steadily, beginning with a trickle, a stream of reinforcements which was shortly to become a torrent began to flow toward East Pakistan. The soldiers wore "civvies" and so attracted no attention. About 30,000 West Pakistani troops were already stationed in the East wing. As the reinforcements flowed across, senior officers scrupulously planned the complex logistics of supplying and equipping an occupying army of 50,000 men from a sailing distance of 3,000 miles. It was calculated that it would take about two months to get the army into a state of full readiness. Unknown to any but the topmost generals in President Yahya's innermost circle, the civil war which was the sole alternative to a return to civilian government had begun.

Meanwhile, the constitutional wrangling continued. Though now sensing, and preparing for, the inevitable showdown, President Yahya nevertheless strove, with what seemed unremitting patience but was more akin to unremitting stealth, to find a way out of the deadlock between Sheikh Mujibur Rahman and Mr. Z. A. Bhutto. Giving no clue that he had already, in his heart, and certainly in his contingency plans, abandoned the scheme on which a nation had pinned its hopes and which 40 million voters, by their personal and very positive act, had underwritten, President Yahya blandly gave a date for the convening of the national assembly. It would meet, he announced, in Dacca on March 3.

Throughout January, talks continued. At the end of the month, the president sought to break out of the constitutional impasse. An almost frenzied series of discussions sent him scurrying backwards and forwards between his capital and Dacca and Karachi. But for all the movement he got nowhere. Sheikh Mujib would not budge from the Six Points.

He would not because he could not. For his massive election victory, which had placed him in so seemingly strong a position, in fact made it impossible for him to compromise. Mujib was trapped in a political vise. Had his victory not been so overwhelming, he would have been able to "sell" a "deal," some compromise, to his supporters. It would have been possible to persuade them that, for the sake of some gains, it was prudent to sacrifice some points of principle. He could even have agreed to go to the assembly without insisting on any of the Six Points at all, knowing that once civilian government had been restored his position would be infinitely more powerful and he would quickly be able to engineer whatever he wanted. In much this way, Singapore's Lee Kuan Yew first joined the Malaysian Federation and then, when he had consolidated his position, broke from it. But, all-powerful and with an absolute majority in the assembly, Mujib could not act in this way. He had an unequivocal mandate not to do so. If he compromised, he would be regarded as having temporized; a "get-out" would be treated as a "sell-out."

But equally there could be no substantial compromise by Mr. Bhutto. In a different way, he was as much the prisoner of circumstances as Sheikh Mujib. For, by winning 81 of its 138 seats, he was now the political leader and voice of West Pakistan, not only of its people but its vested interests. One of these major, supposedly nonpolitical interests, was, of course, the army. Even if Bhutto had been, by belief or nature or political instinct, amenable to making major concessions to Mujib on the Six Points (which he was not), he was totally constrained from doing so.

But apart from those constraints, the Six Points themselves, unless drastically modified (which Mujib's position made impossible), precluded compromise. For they hit at the very basis of Pakistan and hardest of all at the "integrity" which was, in effect, only another name for the very existence of Pakistan as the nation it was. The Six Points envisaged a degree of autonomy for the individual provinces so great that it amounted in effect to something nearer independence than autonomy. For they gave each province—notably East Pakistan—control over its economy and finances, its foreign aid and foreign trade, and even its own militia. And the laxity of federal control which the Six Point program specifically provided implied an unworkably diffuse, almost powerless, central government, whose nominal responsibility for defense was left wholly at the mercy of economic and other policy decisions in the federating provinces. It would, almost certainly, be an unworkable formula in any developing country—and in many developed ones. For Pakistan, given its inborn and acquired strains, it was impossible, and implied the end of Pakistan as one nation.

In this impasse, and finding Mujib inflexible, Bhutto declared on February 17 that it would be pointless for his party to attend the constituent assembly. They had no wish, he said, to make the long flight to Dacca if they could not participate in the framing of a constitution once they got there. The Awami League, however, was preventing this participation, for it was adamant on embodying the Six Points, without modification, in the constitution, and it was in a position, given its majority, to push this through. If the People's Party were denied a hand in the constitution-making, it was a waste of time to attend the assembly. Mujib's rigidity, Bhutto declared, left no room for negotiation. Yet there had to be negotiation if both wings of Pakistan were to frame a national constitution which satisfied the requirements of each.

Bhutto's stand was backed by the smaller West wing parties. Khan Abdul Qayyum Khan, leader of the Qayyum Muslim

League, which had its main strength in the northwest frontier region and nine members in the assembly, said that Mujib's "unbending attitude" would split the country into pieces. He supported provincial autonomy but it must be consistent with a viable central government and must not jeopardize the unity of the nation as a whole.

Mujib answered back, but it was no real answer. At a press conference in Dacca on February 24 he gamely denied that the Six Points would leave the federal government at the mercy of the provinces and said they were designed merely to safeguard provincial autonomy. But this was disingenuous, and he could not explain how this could ever work. Nor, in private conversations, could his legal and constitutional advisers, despite their academic prowess. And this, fundamentally, was because the Six Points were incompatible with a strongly federated Pakistan. As if in recognition that he could not sustain an argument to the contrary, Mujib brusquely dismissed all considered constitutional objections to his program and launched into his familiar diatribe against the West wing. This is not to say his criticisms were unjustified. He fairly claimed that some objections to the Six Points were motivated by the aim of perpetuating East Pakistan's colonial status. The exploitation of East Pakistan had been effected mainly through central government control of foreign aid, foreign trade, and foreign exchange. As a result, the province had become a protected market for the industrialists of West Pakistan and its economy had slid to the edge of collapse. None of this would have happened if foreign aid, trade, and exchange had not been under the control of the center.

Such arguments, in themselves, were unanswerable. President Yahya had himself admitted, more than once, that the East wing had been ill-used, though he had referred to the political rather than the equally evident and more basic economic disparities. But the Sheikh's arguments were unanswerable not only because they were true but because they were based on a wholly different set of premises from those of Mr. Bhutto and others in the West, including, when it came down to it, the president himself. The two sides were speaking two languages far more different than mere Urdu and Bengali. They were really talking about, and taking as axiomatic, two totally different conceptions of Pakistan. And it was not even that their ideas of Pakistan were opposed: they were mutually exclusive. And so the Sheikh's logic, though compelling, was self-defeating—it only made clearer than ever to the leaders of the West that there was no accommodation to be had. But this still did not dawn on the Sheikh and his advisers. They continued to live in a fool's paradise, even as the soldiers oiled their gun barrels, apparently sure that West Pakistan must yield to the will of the majority wing, naively assuming that as the election had been held its verdict would be obeyed. But they had not thought through their slogans to see that the Six Points, which East Pakistan undeniably needed, conflicted in their very essence with the need for a strong federation.

Without a strong federation, or a strong controlling influence at the center of the component parts, the nation would fall apart. For from the very beginning all the conflicting nationalistic impulses in Pakistan had been subsumed in the chimera of an Islamic state. In practical political terms, only a strong central authority could sustain that idea. Only one other new nation in modern times had been founded on the strength of an idea alone, but Israel had several key advantages compared to Pakistan, not least that it was closely knit geographically. Nor did Israel have peoples as contrasted as the Punjabs and Bengalis, to name only two of Pakistan's regional and ethnic varieties, and where there were great differences the variegated Israelis had the great advantage of literacy to bridge the gaps between them.

A strong central authority was vital not only to the continuance of Pakistan as a unit, but to the continuance of West Pakistan too. Without it, not merely would the two wings cease to coexist, but the four provinces of the West would fall apart. Without it, the Punjabis would inevitably outweigh and outrun the other peoples of the West wing, the Sindhis, Baluchis, Pathans, and others, and bring disruption and fragmentation.

A strong federation—if there was to be a return to civil government—was a *sine qua non* for two further crucial reasons. The army, far more than Islam the one cementing force in Pakistan's troubled history, depended for its very existence on the continued integrity of Pakistan. And secondly, this integrity was something to which President Yahya Khan was committed as head of state—and pledged as a man.

12

JUNTA'S SENTENCE

*A man may build himself a throne of bayonets, but
he cannot sit on it*—DEAN INGE

Deadlock was now total. By the third week of February, the
nation had reached the final crisis. All the good will and high
hopes of the election were gone. The army, covertly, was preparing. Nowhere was busier in those last days before disaster
than the army's self-contained cantonments on the edge of
each main town in East Pakistan.

Developments now took on the inexorability of Greek
tragedy. On Sunday, February 21, President Yahya dismissed
his civilian cabinet of ten. A terse announcement from Islamabad said blankly that this was due to "the political situation."

Despite this enigmatic nonexplanation, the meaning was
plain. The army had had enough. The clique of top generals
behind President Yahya Khan no longer disguised their disdain for the experiment in handing back power. The experiment had ignominiously failed, as they always expected it to.
They now saw only one realistic course: abandonment of the
constitutional process coupled with the firmest possible military suppression of the inevitably ensuing Bengali revolt.
Otherwise, they knew, Pakistan would slither into anarchy,
and disintegrate. The generals made their message clear to the
civilian cabinet, who, seeing they had no further role to play
save scapegoat or turncoat, to a man resigned. Simply to save

his own face (always an important consideration in Pakistan), President Yahya took the initiative and sacked them.

It was the first overt step in the tightening of the army's grip on Pakistan. On the same day as the resignation of his cabinet, the president called in all five provincial governors and the martial-law administrators. They were now briefed on how to prepare for the clampdown to come.

A week later, the generals got help from an unexpected quarter. In an emotional outburst, Bhutto, who had already announced that he would boycott the assembly if Mujib did not "modify" the Six Points, now demanded that the 120-day limit on its deliberations be lifted and that the opening session be postponed. If, he declared, the assembly was held as planned on March 3, there would be a total "hartal" (general strike) from the Khyber to Karachi.

To the leadership, fear of insurrection and disorder in West Pakistan was even greater than the threat of rebellion in the East. The President's response was immediate. In a broadcast the following day, March 1, President Yahya confessed that Pakistan now faced "its gravest crisis." Therefore, "with a heavy heart," he had decided to postpone the national assembly meeting indefinitely. This was the only way, he claimed, to allow the political leaders time to find a way out of their deadlock. As the major party of West Pakistan, under Mr. Bhutto, had decided to boycott the assembly, postponement had been forced upon him. No viable and healthy constitution could be drawn up without both wings taking part, and without the West-wing representatives the assemby would be a farce. The President ended his message with a renewed "solemn promise" that he would recall the assembly as soon as conditions were "conducive to constitution-making."

Simultaneously with that "solemn promise," however, the President replaced provincial governors—responsible for running local civil administration—with martial-law officers. And thus the army's grip tightened another notch. More significantly still, Vice-Admiral Ahsan, who had shown great sympathy for Bengali opinion during his two years in office and had built up a considerable rapport with Sheikh Mujib, was quietly replaced with the most unrelenting "hawk" in the en-

tire Pakistan army, General Tikka Khan, the man who was
soon to become the butcher of Bengal. Whatever the President's "solemn promises," the drift of events was unmistakable.
His earlier "solemn promises" to ensure "the transfer of power
to the people," "to protect lives, liberty, and property," "to
put the administration on the rails," to leave East Pakistan's
future "entirely to the wishes of the people," were now equally,
whatever the good intentions that may have prompted them, to
be profligately abandoned. The people were to be denied
power, life itself, and liberty on a scale and with a ruthlessness
not often equaled even in this century.

The response to the President's bombshell came swiftly.
There were violent protests in Dacca, and throughout the East
wing a "hartal" paralyzed normal life for the next five days.
The national flag was publicly burnt and a fresh one unfurled:
the green, red and gold standard of a new "nation": Bangla
Desh as they called it, "Home of the Bengalis" or "Bengal
Nation." Dacca radio broadcast Bengali nationalist songs and
special Bengali news bulletins. Throughout Tuesday, March 2,
workers, students and professional men marched in processions
miles long, chanting through the streets, protesting against the
postponement of the assembly. Nothing now could have
seemed clearer to them than that they had yet again been
cynically cheated of their democratic rights, that yet again the
vested interests of West Pakistan had betrayed the due aspirations of the Bengali people. And, they were convinced, it was
to be the last time. Like the generals, the Bengalis now felt
they had had enough. The cry from every section of the populace, over and over again, was "Bangla Desh, Bangla Desh" and
"Joi Bangla, Joi Bangla, Joi Bangla."

The chaos intensified. All factories, offices, and shops were
closed. A few unfortunates who dared open them were beaten
up by self-appointed vigilantes of the Awami League, an
early ominous sign of the way in which extremists of the movement were to help propel events beyond Mujib's control. The
same fate met anyone driving a car or even riding a bicycle,
and key roads were strewn with rubble, scaffolding, wrecked
cars, and concrete to block traffic. All communications with
the outside world, and particularly West Pakistan, were dis-

rupted or cut altogether. But the army kept to its cantonments.

All the pent-up bitterness and hatred for West Pakistan now welled up into an ugly xenophobia which spared no one who was not a Bengali and even brought death by mischance to some who were. At the airport, normal services were canceled and thousands of West Pakistanis, fearing for their lives as Bengal boiled over, camped in the airport building with their terror-stricken families and dark bundles of belongings, in the hope of escape. The waiting list topped 3,000 by March 5 and thousands more were applying. In a situation of mounting chaos, foreign diplomatic missions began arrangements to evacuate their nationals in emergency aircraft specially flown in. When the planes arrived, they had to land without being "talked in," as the airport's ground staff were on strike. Unable to reply any longer on normal means of communication, diplomats prepared to keep in touch with one another from their homes by shortwave radio. At the Intercontinental, Dacca's only modern hotel, guests were ordered to stay in their rooms and not look out of the windows. The restaurant, bar, and swimming pool were closed on Awami League orders: if the hated non-Bengalis (mainly Europeans and Americans) staying at the hotel could not be hurt, at least they could be made uncomfortable. All English language signs were blanked out or destroyed, and throughout the city students and workers and hoodlums angrily roamed the streets tearing down signs in English and Urdu, looting the non-Bengali-owned stores and burning cars. The protests quickly brought on more serious violence. Hundreds were wounded in street clashes and Dacca's main hospital reported sixteen deaths on the hartal's first day. In Chittagong there were worse scenes: Punjabi factory managers and others were burnt alive, publicly beheaded, disemboweled, or dragged along behind moving vehicles, their heads smashing to pulp along the potholed roads. The death tolls multiplied a hundredfold during the week as the Bengali mobs, incensed and hysterical now, hardly caring who they hurt or what they damaged, and defying a martial-law curfew, went on the rampage. For that week, a pattern was set: an eerie paralysis by day broken only by the incantations of the massed demonstrators, and mob rule by night. By the weekend, March 6, some 3,000 people had been killed. But only a few by the army, for throughout this time, by clearly prearranged plan, the army hardly stirred from the cantonments. The soldiers attempted only a few law-enforcing forays with small contingents, and these were ineffectual. Of the 3,000 killed that week, the army was probably responsible for fewer than 300. The Bengali mobs seethed excitedly in the army's absence, failing to sense that it was deliberate. Fantasizing as ever they deluded themselves that by some miracle they had already won independence. Foreign observers, however, and others less heady with nationalist fervor, saw what was obvious: the generals were holding back, choosing their time, making sure they were fully ready and, above all, giving the Bengalis a scaffold's length of rope, ensuring that the wave of Bengali excesses and the collapse of administration would provide the army with every excuse to wade in and "restore order." So the soldiers stayed quietly in the cantonments. Two army helicopters (one more than could be made available in November for cyclone relief) patrolled over the city and they were the only clear sign that the army was on the watch.

Sheikh Mujib, however, was too astute not to see the dangers clearly. He was always the most moderate in his party. He had, of course, denounced the assembly postponement in violent terms, and he had called the hartal. He could do no less. But now he also succeeded in curbing his wider and more extreme supporters, and saw to it that essential services again began to run properly. In effect, he set up a parallel government. The banks were to open to pay wages and the shops to sell food. Meanwhile, he rejected an invitation from President Yahya Khan to a round-table conference with Mr. Bhutto and leaders of the smaller parties. It was, he said, "an invitation at gunpoint."

Faced with open defiance of his authority yet still, perhaps, clinging to the hope that he could salvage something from the wreckage, President Yahya came again to the microphones on Saturday, March 6. He purported to be pained and surprised by Mujib's reply, although Mujib could hardly have spoken otherwise. He blamed "the forces of disorder" for exploiting the situation. Then, although Pakistan's political condition was now much worse and the constitutional deadlock no better than when he had postponed the assembly indefinitely, the president suddenly yielded. He declaimed in bulldog tones: "I cannot wait indefinitely," and then announced a concession. The assembly would meet after all, on March 25. It seemed like a capitulation to pressure from the "forces of disorder." However, there came a string of ominous warnings. "No matter what happens, as long as I am in command, I will ensure the complete and absolute integrity of Pakistan. Let there be no doubt or mistake on this point. I have a duty toward millions of people of East and West Pakistan to preserve this country. I will not allow a handful of people to destroy the homeland of millions."

The president had again misjudged, just as he had misjudged one cyclone crisis in November. East Pakistan was in no mood to be bullied, and the bulldog tones had the ring of challenge. More than 70 million Bengalis were now united as never before and were no mere "handful." Not only that: Mujib had won the election. It was true the president had given way to pressure by setting a new date for the assembly, but his speech appeared to give reassurances only to the parties of West Pakistan. For the president told them they had "nothing to fear" from the constitution-making process because "there was no better assurance than the provisions of the Legal Framework Order." This, of course, stipulated that Pakistan must have a strong central government and must retain federal unity: exactly what Mr. Bhutto was demanding, exactly the point where the East-West deadlock centered. Bhutto, of course, had every right to his demand. But in East Pakistan—Bangla Desh as it was becoming more and more familiarly known—it now simply seemed as if President Yahya had become a paid-up member of the People's Party. He had said nothing that could convince the Bengalis that there was any hope left for them but a unilateral declaration of the independence of Bangla Desh.

The president's speech did even further damage. It strengthened suspicion that he was now no longer in control even at Islamabad and had become a mere catspaw of the inner clique of "hawkish" generals. For on March 1 President Yahya had placed the main blame for breakdown on Mr. Bhutto. On March 6, however, the blame had shifted "particularly" to Sheikh Mujibur Rahman. And in the same speech were two totally different tones: the one that averred yet again the president's faith in the constitution-making process and his struggle to find a way out of the impasse; and the one that threatened to use armed force to insure "national integrity"—which to Bengalis meant the denial of the autonomy they had voted for. And they asked: if the president is not in control, who is? It could only be the generals.

President Yahya Khan was indeed now speaking with two voices. For he was caught in a terrible dilemma. There was the voice of democracy but it was the voice also of unreason, for democracy could not work in this utterly divided nation— because, above all, it was divided. And there was the voice of authority, which was also the voice of logic, for it alone could keep Pakistan together, by sheer brute force.

Why, then, did President Yahya not bring the army in, or why had he not done so earlier? It seemed extraordinary that all through the turmoil in East Pakistan in the first week of March, the army stayed in barracks. It was as if the martial-law regime had surreptitiously abdicated.

The government, in fact, was not fully resolute. The generals had no doubts that armed suppression of the Bengali autonomist movement was the only course. But the president resisted them, holding out against the "final solution"—this echo of the Nazi holocaust was soon to seem apt in East Pakistan. This was partly because he was basically a humane man who understood, and cared, how enormous the cost would be in human terms, but it was primarily because he had pledged himself to and identified himself with a transfer of power to a popularly elected government. Naturally, he held out as long as possible against admitting defeat.

And there was another, even more important, factor in the holding back of the army. The generals had been hampered in their buildup of their East Pakistan garrisons by a dispute with India which had cut one of Pakistan's lifelines: the air-lanes over India between the two wings. Earlier in the year, an Indian Airlines plane had been hijacked from Srinagar, capital of India-held Kashmir, to Lahore in West Pakistan. The hijackers claimed to be anti-Indian "freedom fighters" and were given a heroes' welcome in Pakistan. The plane itself was blown up under the noses of the Pakistan authorities, who refused to compensate the Indian government. As a result, India banned all Pakistan overflights, which compelled the Pakistanis to fly their aircraft right around the southern tip of India, trebling the journey between East and West wings. This, of course, prolonged the reinforcing and equipping of units, 30,-000 strong already, stationed in East Pakistan. Ironically, the hijacking incident, which the Pakistanis had at first welcomed, cost them dear, in time and money, and the hijackers, heroes for the day, were later denounced as Indian agents, and incarcerated.

But by March 6 the buildup had been going on for weeks. There were now 20,000 more West-wing soldiers in East Pakistan, highly trained, well-equipped, and thoroughly indoctrinated in dogmas of race hatred, regarding Bengalis as traitors, inferiors, and India lovers: "deserving" to be butchered. The army was almost ready.

13

STAY OF EXECUTION

The smiler with the knife under the cloak.—
CHAUCER

As President Yahya Khan, in his serverest pseudo-Sandhurst
tones, lectured the nation from Islamabad that Saturday,
March 6, Sheikh Mujibur Rahman and his lieutenants listened
intently in the barely furnished rooms of the Sheikh's house
in Dacca. As soon as the broadcast ended, they went into con-
clave, and they were not to emerge for another nine hours. For
they now had to make the most crucial decisions they had ever
faced. All Bengal (Indian and Pakistani) awaited the declaration of an independent Bangla Desh. The mood of nationalist
euphoria was paramount: few gave thought to the Sheikh's
repeated warnings that a million more lives might have to be
lost in the fight for independence. In twenty-four more hours
the Sheikh was to address a mass audience in Dacca and it was
widely rumored that he would proclaim the new nation's birth.
But the Awami League's executive committee had harsh decisions to face. Were they to take the onus of responsibility for
declaring independence? Was the blood of a million Bengalis
to be on their hands? Or should they back away from the
brink? If so, could they?—Would their supporters allow
them to? Their task that day was to decide what the Sheikh
must tell his people.

It was the Sheikh himself who urged the moderate course,

and got his way. He strove to disabuse his hotter-headed officers of their political delusions. East Pakistan, he insisted, would gain nothing from secession except bloodshed and torment. If the army could not bludgeon its way to control, the ensuing turmoil would open the way to anarchy or communism or an amalgam of both. Whatever way it went, it would be the people in whose name they were acting who would suffer, and suffer appallingly. The only course, the Sheikh still believed, was somehow to remain a part of Pakistan. That was the only chance East Pakistan stood of clawing back at least some of the resources and funds the West had extracted. In any event, Sheikh Mujib argued, the Awami League's mandate was not for independence, but for autonomy. If they now exceeded that mandate by a unilateral act, it would be a defiance of President Yahya's internationally recognized regime, and they would therefore forfeit any chance of outside aid or recognition.

These were telling points. After hours of discussion, the hardliners who had wanted an outright leap for independence were defeated. But the Sheikh and his men knew only too well how difficult it would be to "sell" anything less than independence to the wildly enthusiastic masses on the following afternoon. Wrangling late into the night, they devised the formula which enabled Mujib to stop short of the brink but yet retain the loyalty of the Bengalis.

But Mujib's formula was one which attempted the impossible. Dressed up in the plumage of Bengali rhetoric, it fired the spirit of half a million listeners as much as an outright independence declaration would have done. In that it was a gesture of defiance, it was what they wanted. But it was a gesture only. What Mujib did was to refuse to attend the assembly unless four main conditions were met. President Yahya must withdraw martial law. The soldiers "must return to barracks." There must be an inquiry into army killings in East Pakistan, officially admitted a week later to total 172. And power must be transferred to the elected representatives of the people. Later Mujib added a fifth demand, that reinforcements of army units from West Pakistan must cease. Until the demands were met, there would be a mass campaign

of civil disobedience. The hartal would cease but no government offices, universities, schools, or courts were to open.
No taxes or other government revenue should be paid. Banking transactions with West Pakistan were stopped and the
assets of West-wing firms frozen.

The Awami League's preconditions now totalled eleven:
the Six Points and the five demands. It was clear that only
consummate political bargaining of a kind never yet seen in
Pakistan could save the nation from disaster. However, the
certainty of that disaster logically followed, for there was no
scope for such negotiation, even if the negotiators had been
up to it. Mujib's demands were either empty or unfulfillable.
The president could not end martial law without resigning and
admitting complete capitulation at a stroke. The demand for
the soldiers to return to barracks was mere rhetoric: despite
the shootings of the past week, the army had, by and large,
held back in the face of massive civil disruption and repeated
outright defiance of every basic martial law regulation, including the curfew. An inquiry into army killings was a point of
little substance—a sop to mass feeling. And the fourth pre-
condition of the March 7 speech, that power be transferred to
the people's elected representatives *before* the Awami League
would attend the assembly, begged the whole question. That
two such speeches as Sheikh Mujib's and President Yahya's
could be made that weekend was a measure of the depth of
crisis into which Pakistan had sunk. "There is still time for
us to live as brothers if things are settling peacefully," said
Mujib plaintively. He was whistling in the dark. The nation
was going inexorably down now into the quicksand.

Again the Awami League launched a mass campaign of
disruption. In almost everything but name, East Pakistan now
became a separate nation—even the judges, the quintessential
symbol of national authority, went on strike, and General
Tikka Khan, the new governor, could find no one to swear
him into office. The paralysis of normal administration, the
cessation of all normal commercial and economic activity
made life very difficult. Most people in East Pakistan live a
hand-to-mouth existence, but now the chronic economic crisis
was compounded. Food prices soared as essentials became

scarce: potatoes were selling for a rupee (22 cents) each, and even rice, the staple diet, went up 20 percent in a week. With factories closed, workers could earn no money and even the comparatively wealthy, those with bank accounts, could not draw on them. But the squeeze was more than financial: because the ports were closed and the airport clogged, hospitals began to run out of vital medicines. Meanwhile, the foreign community, diplomatic missions, and relief agencies, on whom many thousands of Bengalis depended in various ways for their lives and living, began their own mass evacuation. Most of the 900 British in East Pakistan were flown out on specially chartered aircraft, leaving their tea estates, businesses, cloth mills, and other concerns, employing thousands of people, to grind to a halt. Germans, Belgians, and Americans got out too. U Thant ordered the families of UN personnel to leave, and various aid and relief agencies gave up in despair. It had been some weeks since they had been able to continue their work in the cyclone-stricken area in the south of the province, but now they could not even get to their offices in Dacca to do the paperwork. So 3,000,000 helpless people in the cyclone area alone were left to fend for themselves, and all over East Pakistan thousands of others, fleeing from the towns, took to roaming the countryside in search of shelter and food.

As in 1969, Sheikh Mujib demonstrated that his qualities of leadership could cross the bounds of mere polemic. Despite the pressure from the student extremists on whom his party depended for its dynamic, he succeeded, day by day, in bringing the situation slowly under a greater measure of control, gradually allowing shops to open, banks to conduct essential transactions, and commerce to get going again, albeit on far too small a scale to mitigate the chaos and hardship. It was a skillful job of organization and orchestration in a tricky political situation. In this, Mujib's closest aide was Tajuddin Ahmed.

Now, if ever, the Awami League leadership demonstrated that it had East Pakistan in its palm. It patently had the right to govern. But in what framework? Maulana Bashani, far to the left of Mujib, saw clearly that "the time has come to sacrifice blood" and he told a rally in Dacca on March 10 that there was no room for compromise. Only the persuasively sensible influence of Begum Mujibur Rahman deterred the Maulana from calling outright for an immediate mass insurrection, and he committed his National Awami Party to form a front with the Awami League. But Bashani's ideas for the framework in which Mujib would rule were not Mujib's ideas and they most certainly were not the president's ideas. So yet again, the two most important men in Pakistan, President Yahya and Sheikh Mujib, wrestled with the political and constitutional complexities which beset their nation, to save it from the abyss.

The president made it known that he would again go to Dacca for talks with Mujib: had he been less sincere or less determined to find a solution, or more a man to insist on protocol, he would surely have demanded that for once Mujib should come to him. So now hopes mounted slightly that they could reach some compromise. To informed observers, it seemed more likely than otherwise that Mujib and the president were both anxious to prevent East Pakistan from descending into an anarchy from which only extremists could benefit. There was talk of some interim government which would end martial law but keep Yahya as president. It was attractive talk but glib thinking. The mood in East Pakistan was far less rosy when the president flew into Dacca and rapidly drove, under heavy armed guard, to his high-walled villa near the Intercontinental Hotel. On the day he arrived, Mujib emphasized the realities of the situation by issuing thirty-five directives, many of which flew in the face of martial-law orders, including orders to key workers in government defense factories to stay at home—an offense punishable by ten years' rigorous imprisonment. And Mujib pushed the point home by announcing: "The president will be our guest"—a subtle indication of East Pakistan's *de facto* independence. Under increasing mass pressure, the Awami League was slipping into more extreme and provocative postures. Hopes for a successful outcome to the meeting could hardly have had a flimsier base, despite the conjectures of informed observers. The first sign that the discussions were going badly came on March 18, after three days of negotiation, when Sheikh Mujib

flatly rejected the president's offer to set up an inquiry into
the army shootings earlier in the month. The demand for an
inquiry was one of the four preconditions which Mujib set
in his March 7 speech. Now, however, he said the president's
proposed terms of reference for the inquiry would prevent it
from investigating "atrocities." He also objected to its operating under martial law. Another of Mujib's demands, that the
army "withdraw to barracks," had already been met in full,
so it was now clear that of the four demands Mujib originally
had made, the two which could be met had been. But that did
not affect the situation in the slightest, because the demands
were empty in the first place. Mujib's purported objection to
the inquiry's terms of reference was simply his smokescreen.
As ever, he was the prisoner of his supporters and was constantly having to appease them.

What went on behind the smokescreen in the ornately
furnished lounges of the presidential villa was quite another
matter. For despite the Sheikh's hard words, which were (as
President Yahya well knew) solely for his gallery, and despite
even an incident on March 19, the fourth day of talks, when
soldiers killed twenty civilians in an unexplained clash near
Dacca, he was clearly searching for a compromise. Sheikh
Mujib knew, if no one else in his party did, that compromise
was the only course if moderate policies were to prevail on
either side, if East Pakistan was to stand any chance at all of
recovering some of what it had lost to the West over twenty-
three years, if the Maoists and anarchists and other extremists
waiting in the wings were not to swamp the stage. His problem,
as he explained to Yahya, was to "sell" that compromise. And
the president seemed to understand, though by now he had
rightly concluded that the Awami League was slithering un-
controllably leftwards. But for a spell, on March 19 or 20,
the two men found their way through to what might have
seemed a "salable" formula: one that the generals could accept from Yahya, one that the students could accept from
Mujib. Its full nature has never been reliably disclosed, but
in essence it was this: the assembly would meet in Dacca as
arranged; there would be no constitutional preconditions but
each wing would produce its own constitution for a consensus

to be reached in the assembly; and President Yahya would continue as head of state. The president, Bengali leaders and Mr. Bhutto have all since given their own very differing versions of this tentative agreement, but whatever it was no longer matters. It could never possibly have worked. Each leader now was simply clutching at straws and, in Yahya's case, simultaneously biding his time.

The unexpected "progress" (it was never more than a chimera) led the president to call Bhutto over from Karachi to join the talks. Bhutto was now the devil incarnate for the Bengalis—the man whose threats had led the president to postpone the assembly. A savagely hostile demonstration greeted him on arrival. He had to be heavily escorted by armed bodyguards, and at the Intercontinental Hotel was jeered even by the normally deferential, self-effacing staff. He had the fright of his life when the lift doors jammed for three minutes and he had to stand confronting a pushing, angry crowd, prevented from lynching him only by a phalanx of gunmen. The talks with Sheikh Mujib and President Yahya on the following day, March 22, were the first that the three men had held together. The false hopes of the 20th were quickly dashed and the discussions degenerated into haggling. There was only one point on which they could agree, a further postponement of the inaugural assembly meeting, due on March 25. The ostensible reason for this was, in President Yahya's words, to "facilitate and enlarge the area of agreement among the political parties." But by now the pretense that a political solution was going to be possible had worn through. There was no area of agreement to be enlarged. The only wonder is that Sheikh Mujib seemed not to realize how near to nemesis he was—or perhaps he had passed the point of caring. In many ways, he might have reasoned, it would be easier to become a martyr than to spend a futile lifetime wrestling with the impossible problems of his homeland and its people.

The brink was reached. March 23, Pakistan's "Republic Day," was declared "Resistance Day" in East Pakistan, a tactless and provocative gesture of defiance by the Awami League. Mujib issued a "declaration of emancipation" which really meant nothing: while averring yet again that bullets, guns, and bayonets would not cow the Bengalis, it was more a matter of sound and fury than a message of significance. Mujib was still going through the motions of being all things to all men, satisfying his supporters with slogans and, simultaneously, trying to achieve some sort of accord with the regime. But the very conception of "Resistance Day" was a flagrant taunt to West-wing military authority, and it was more than merely foolhardy. It was a deliberate bid by the hardliners in Mujib's camp to sabotage any prospects of a "deal." And as hundreds of "Bangla Desh" flags went up all over Dacca, above homes, shops, schools, and public buildings, and above Mujib's own house, the considered provocation of the regime was compounded by the public burning of Jinnah's portrait and of the Pakistan national flag outside Mujib's home, with Mujib himself present. It was a gross error on Mujib's part to expose himself so openly to the charge of treason. Awami League publications, also, were now openly insulting and seditious. There had to come a point when even President Yahya's tolerance would snap, and it seemed the deliberate aim of many leading Bengalis, not least the intellectuals who did the Awami League's thinking, to push toward that point. They doubtless reasoned true and saw no hope, need, or purpose in any reconciliation with the West wing. Certainly, too—though the Bengalis could not know this—the generals had already decided to crack down. But it was foolish and reckless of the Bengali leadership and intelligentsia to help push the nation over the brink, for it involved scant thought beyond vainglorious daydreams of how retribution would be wrought.

14

MILITARY VENGEANCE

Happy be the bounteous realm.—Opening words of Pakistan's national anthem

"Retribution" proved savage. On March 25, without another word to Mujib, the president and Bhutto returned to Karachi. Bhutto complained on arrival that the Sheikh had shown "no sign of reciprocity" (which was untrue) and that the degree of autonomy he demanded was more than autonomy, it bordered on sovereignty (which was all too true). Mujib, meanwhile, spent these last few hours of freedom exhorting large crowds in Dacca to prepare for "supreme sacrifice," and issued a despairing last series of orders designed, now that all chance of settlement was gone, to sever the East wing from West Pakistan. Then, wearily, resigned, he went to his home to await the inevitable. Most of his senior Awami League colleagues, lacking the stuff of martyrs, were busily fleeing toward the border and the sanctuary of India.

That night, the holocaust began.

But for the resource and daring, far beyond the call of duty, of two journalists, the horrors that passed in Dacca that night would even now be undocumented. For as part of their long-prepared plan, the generals intended to conceal from the world what they were about to do. Army officers moved into the Intercontinental Hotel a few hours before the soldiers were unleashed and rounded up the corps of foreign journalists staying there. They were taken to the airport on the edge of the city, locked in a room, rudely stripped of all notes and documents, and flown out to Karachi the following morning, where they were stripped and searched again. But two journalists, Michel Laurent, a French photographer working for the Associated Press news agency, and Simon Dring, of the *Daily Telegraph* of London, resourcefully evaded the net. In his report, Dring gave the first eyewitness account of the terror campaign which Pakistan's leaders had designed to "save" the "integrity" of their nation. "The first targets as the tanks rolled into Dacca," Dring reported, "were the students. Caught completely by surprise, some two hundred students were killed in Iqbal Hall, headquarters of the militantly antigovernment students' union, as shells slammed into the building and their rooms were sprayed with machine-gun fire. Two days later, bodies were still smoldering in their burning rooms, others were scattered outside and more floated in a nearby lake. Seven teachers died in their quarters and a family of twelve were gunned down as they hid in an outhouse. The military removed many of the bodies but the sixty still there could never have accounted for all the blood in Iqbal Hall. At another hall, the dead were buried by the soldiers in a hastily dug mass grave and then bulldozed over by tanks."

But this was only a small part of the army's action that night. Later, government propagandists claimed that the University had become the headquarters of rabid secessionists who were heavily armed and were plotting a violent insurrection. But no corresponding excuse has ever been offered for what followed the attack on the University, doubtless for the simple reason that none, not even the most far-fetched, is conceivable. Dring estimated that three battalions of troops, one armored, one artillery, and one infantry, went into the attack on Dacca. Within three hours of the onslaught's beginning, fires were burning all over the city. Opposite the Intercontinental Hotel, a platoon stormed the empty offices of an Awami League newspaper and burned it down, along with most houses in the area. But they reserved their fiercest attack for the Hindu area of the old town. "There, the soldiers made the people come out of their houses and then just shot them in groups." This area, like many others, was razed.

After a night of terror, there was worse to come. Dring continued: "Shortly before dawn most firing had stopped and . . . an eerie silence settled over the city. . . . At mid-day, again without any warning, columns of troops poured into the old section of the city where more than a million people live in a sprawling maze of narrow, winding streets. For the next 11 hours they proceeded systematically to devastate large areas of the old town, where Sheikh Mujib had some of his strongest support. . . ." Whole areas were flattened, hundreds of dwellings burned, their occupants shot, burned, and raped, and for two days the pogrom continued. Dring and Laurent estimated that the army slaughtered 7,000 people in Dacca during these two days and nights. "People are still being shot at the slightest provocation," Dring wrote. "Buildings are still being indiscriminately destroyed. It is impossible to assess what all this has so far cost in terms of innocent human lives. But reports beginning to filter in from the outlying areas, Chittagong, Comilla, and Jessore, put the figure, including Dacca, in the region of 15,000 dead."

Simon Dring's remarkable report shattered official Pakistan efforts to stifle the truth. Government spokesmen were reduced to making the absurd claim that he had "made it up," or had not even been there, or did not even exist. The leadership had banked on hiding its policies of massacre by the most rigorous censorship. But it was a bid as futile as it was despicable. The generals' policy was clearly to "solve" the East Pakistan problem once and for all, by launching a campaign of such brutal suppression that the Bengalis would be cowed and terrorized into quiescence forever. This policy was underwritten in the weeks to come throughout West Pakistan as the army carefully sought out and liquidated students, teachers, journalists, lawyers, doctors, businessmen, and other Bengali professional men, aiming to smash the intellectual kernel—the future—of the Bengali national movement. And when that was accomplished, the soldiers, under orders and with the direct encouragement of senior officers—for otherwise it could not have happened—vented sheer bloodlust on the 10 million Hindus of East Pakistan. Yet within two days of beginning this terror campaign, the regime was busily claiming that East Pakistan was returning to "normal." During the summer, evidence mounted sky-high to the contrary and new evidence piled on old evidence. The leadership's only counter was to blind itself to the realities. President Yahya and his men took refuge in the pretense that the regime had become the victim of international conspiracy to libel it and so continued, unswervingly and shamelessly, in defiance of a mass of detailed and amply confirmed reports of the atrocities committed in their name, to pursue their task of crushing a nation of more than 70 million people.

East Pakistan was now, irrevocably, Bangla Desh in the hearts of its people, however crushed. But they began to pay the price for the lack of realism of *their* leaders. They had woefully underestimated the weight with which the army would crack down. Now, they were simply stunned, and, of course, bereft of leadership. It was months before Bengalis, both in Pakistan and in India, where also Bengalis identified themselves with the Bangla Desh movement, could bring themselves to admit that Sheikh Mujibur Rahman was no longer at their head.

What happened to him was recorded by Simon Dring in his *Daily Telegraph* report of March 29. Mujib had steadfastly refused the entreaties of his supporters to escape. It is highly doubtful that escape was ever possible: his house, down a suburban lane, was certainly carefully watched and was easily sealed off. Soon after 1 A.M. a contingent of soldiers in armored vehicles and trucks drove into the narrow road and fired over the house. "Sheikh, you should come down," an officer called out, in English. Mujib came onto the first floor balcony and replied: "Yes, I am ready. But there is no need to fire. All you need to have done was call me on the telephone and I would have come." He was taken away. For weeks there was no news: he could have been dead. But in June, President Yahya disclosed that he was in prison at a remote place in West Pakistan, and in July announced that he would be put on trial for his life on charges of high treason.

Such was the bankruptcy of the "case" against Mujib that

the regime was even sinking to the expedient of using the "Agartala conspiracy" smear all over again. A government "White Paper" issued some months later, in August, claimed that Mujib had been treasonably plotting with India since 1967, an absurd charge. But President Yahya Khan had already grossly prejudged the issue. For in a speech on the radio on March 26 he denounced Mujib's noncooperation movement as "an act of treason" and Mujib and his party as "enemies of Pakistan" whose "crime will not go unpunished." This extraordinary and dishonest broadcast rang the death knell of the "integrity" of Pakistan, for "punishment" of the movement which had won most of the votes in December not only spelled the end of any voluntary union between the two wings, it also finished any claims, as to the "integrity" of President Yahya Khan as a national leader.

The president gave a detailed account of his discussions with Sheikh Mujib and Mr. Bhutto. The Sheikh, had said, had proposed that martial law be withdrawn and the assembly sit in two committees, one West, one East. The president said that the plan had serious legal and other flaws. Nevertheless he was "prepared to agree" to it in principle if Mr. Bhutto and the other party leaders also agreed.

But it turned out that they did not, for the scheme was bound to split the nation, and he "entirely agreed" with them. On the evening of March 23, they came to him and said they had tried to persuade Mujib to change his stand, but he would not budge.

Then, abruptly, without explanation, the president launched into an angry *non sequitur:* "Sheikh Mujibur Rahman's action in starting his noncooperation movement is an act of treason. He and his party have defied lawful authority for over three weeks. They have insulted Pakistan's flag and defiled the photograph of the Father of the Nation. They have tried to run a parallel government. They have created terror, turmoil, and insecurity. Millions of our Bengali brethren and those who have settled in East Pakistan are living in a state of panic. The armed forces located in East Pakistan have been submitted to taunts and insults of all kinds."

The diatribe went on: "I should have taken action against

Sheikh Mujibur Rahman and his collaborators weeks ago, but I had to try my utmost to handle the situation in such a manner as not to jeopardize my plan of peaceful transfer of power. In my eagerness to achieve this aim I kept on tolerating one illegal act after another, and at the same time I explored every possible avenue for arriving at some reasonable solution." But, alleged the president, Mujib had failed to respond in any constructive way. On the contrary, the Awami League had flouted governmental authority even when the president was in Dacca. "Mujib's obstinacy, obduracy, and absolute refusal to talk sense can lead to but one conclusion—the man and his party are enemies of Pakistan and want East Pakistan to break away completely from the country. He has attacked the solidarity and integrity of this country—the crime will not go unpunished. We will not allow some power-hungry and unpatriotic people to destroy this country and play with the destiny of 120 million people." The president had therefore ordered the army to restore the authority of the government. Meanwhile, his main aim was still to transfer power to the elected representatives of the people.

In a series of new martial-law orders, the Awami League was outlawed, all political activity totally banned throughout Pakistan, complete press censorship imposed, all government employees in East Pakistan ordered to return to work and an indefinite curfew imposed in the East wing.

President Yahya Khan's speech was a farrago of evasive half-truths. As in his earlier broadcasts, he seemed to be speaking with two voices. The speech had the ring of a man who had given up the struggle to be true either to himself or to the facts, a man who, defeated by the political and constitutional complexities—indeed, impossibilities—could not bring himself to admit that, like Hitler, his "patience was exhausted," above all could not admit that his policy was one of suppressing the majority of his "brethren" in the name of a minority. He took refuge in "patriotism"—as ever, the refuge of the scoundrel. There was much truth in the president's castigation of the Awami League's defiant postures of the past few weeks: These were grave sins of political ill-judgment in the East wing, but they did not excuse a retaliation of indiscriminate mass "punishment." Nor did they merit the description of Mujib as "traitor": whatever it was, it could hardly be treason to insist on the Six Points which he had been elected to carry through. Moreover, East Pakistan was the majority wing. If a national split was to be termed a "breakaway," it was simply topsy-turvy to describe East Pakistan as the wing that was breaking away. And if Mujib were suddenly guilty of treason, then President Yahya stood guilty of treachery, for he had treated with the traitor. He had even been "prepared to agree" to the "traitor's" proposals. President Yahya's special pleading simply did not hang together. By the time he spoke, the soldiers had already begun to "restore the authority of the government"— by killing near to 10,000 people, in the most ferocious manner, and by long-prepared plan, of which President Yahya had all along full knowledge. There lay the base and basic insincerity of the president's message. His speech was a tissue of rationalization for what was intended to be the unknown and unreported butchery of the Bengal people and for the steps taken to achieve it at the very time that the president still purported to be seeking a political solution.

For this, President Yahya Khan deserves to be condemned. It is doubtful, all the same, that he had any real choice. There are those, particularly in India (where hardly anyone can think straight on Pakistan), who say his whole policy was an elaborate ruse, that he never intended to hand over power to freely elected politicians. For this, there is no evidence; it is mere surmise. Like most conspiracy theories, it is more interesting than realistic, and implies a degree of dissimulation on Yahya's part that strains reason. This much is clear: if President Yahya never meant what he said, in all his many declarations of avowed intent, he had missed his vocation; he should have been an actor. His broadcast came two years to the day after his original promise to provide a "sound, clean, and honest" basis for a return to civilian government, only one year after his announcement of the Legal Framework Order which was to be the foundation of "a new, fair, happier Pakistan." Everything President Yahya had said, until the latest phase, bore the stamp of sincerity—and, more important by far, not only what he said but what he did. It is doubtful if he could have so fooled not only the electorate and the politicians but also the civilian cabinet of ten who advised him at every stage along the way.

What really went wrong went wrong years before. It was simply that the president's plan was unworkable and it was unworkable because Pakistan was unworkable. For the reasons we have seen, there never could have been a real, lasting political solution. In this context, whether the Yahya master plan was a sham or not hardly matters. Hindsight now suggests that the hardline generals had counted on December's election producing a confused result, with no party—and certainly not the Awami League—paramount. A handover to the politicians would then have been demonstrably impossible, and so power would remain in their hands anyway. And, perhaps, when that calculation went awry, with the unexpectedly clear-cut election result, the generals decided to take the law into their own hands. Certainly, as a body, they were unsympathetic to the whole notion of a democratic Pakistan. As an elite, they took an elitist view; as a military aristocracy in a rigidly stratified society, they were deeply contemptous of "mobocracy," which to them was what democracy meant. And they certainly saw their whole future threatened by a handover to civilian rule. Nevertheless, the available evidence, including the testimony to me of a Bengali member of the civilian cabinet, indicates that the generals were ready to give full parliamentary democracy a chance if, and only if, the army's position and privileges were not jeopardized. But when it became plain so soon that the politicians would not be able to make it work, the generals did step smartly in. To this, President Yahya himself may or may not have been a willing accomplice. According to his lights, he was not—but he was an accomplice willy-nilly. For whatever the election result had been, the outcome for Pakistan would sooner or later have had to be the same: only some extrapolitical agency could keep the two wings together. And what else could do the job but the army? So, in one way or another, in one form or another—either direct, through brute strength and martial law, or more subtly, through the medium of pliant politicians—the army was bound to continue ruling Pakistan. Otherwise, Pakistan would cease to be Pakistan. And it was this, ultimately, which brought about President Yahya's complicity. The reasons for his action suggested by the conspiracy theories, that he was a double-dyed villain all along or a mere creature of the malevolent cabal of top generals, are needlessly complicated. The truth, simple and awful, was that President Yahya Khan genuinely thought he could solve the problem of Pakistan. But he found it was too big for him, in fact insoluble, and found too that he was torn between his conscience as a man and his duty as a president.

When he realized that his answer was wrong, he chose duty, and then opted for the only answer that did meet the case, gruesome as it was. (And had to opt so—simply to resign would have been unsoldierly.) It was not, perhaps, so strange. After all, Sheikh Mujib had warned his Bengalis that they might have to sacrifice a million lives to win their nation; President Yahya took a similar, though less heroic, decision: to take those Bengali lives to save *his* nation. It was the other side of the medal. Given that his duty was to defend the nation's very existence, the alternative the president had to bludgeoning Bangla Desh was, by that criterion, even worse— the ultimate defeat, the abandonment of the East wing, the end of Pakistan. President Yahya Khan was, therefore, not the first "honorable" man in history propelled into "dishonorable" courses. That cannot absolve him from responsibility for the horrendous consequences. But just as a fundamentally peaceable Lincoln had to take his nation into a ruinous civil war in order to save it, so President Yahya Khan had to force the East wing to heel.

15

BANGLA DESH

Indifference to the present characterizes every branch of the Indian intellect; . . . to subjugate the understanding and exalt the imagination is the universal principle.—HENRY THOMAS BUCKLE

Despite their long and careful preparations, the generals' plans misfired. It had clearly been their aim to quickly crush the Bengalis by the massive use of force and terror methods, and then set the country on its feet again. This plan recoiled. For the military elite never had any conception of the strength of Bengali feeling, nor the faintest idea of the determined spirit that would inspire the Bangla Desh resistance movement. This was hardly surprising. They had always been divorced from the basic human realities of the East wing, as they showed so glaringly after the November cyclone. So, the army was able to stun Dacca into sullen submission, but no more. Within three days the city was quiet—too quiet. The regime claimed that everything was returning swiftly to normal, that the "miscreants" and "criminal elements" had been taken care of. But that "normality" was no more than the absence of activity: it was the normality of the graveyard. Tens of thousands had fled Dacca; thousands were dead. Those who remained had no choice but to carry on as best they could, under the heel of the occupying army. Insofar as fighting subsided, things were "normal"; otherwise, not.

And elsewhere in the province the army met quite un-
anticipated resistance. There were battles in almost every
town: Comilla, Khulna, Rangpur, Dinajpur, Rajshani, Bogra,
Sylhet, Jessore, Chittagong, and others. The army was merciless in its bid to eliminate opposition. Bombing and strafing
from the air and its vastly superior fire power and sheer military know-how on the ground made its ultimate victory certain. It was never really a civil war, for the army was too
dominant. In military terms, Bengali resistance was minuscule.
Bengalis are not, like the Pathans and Punjabis who tore into
them, at all a martial people. Their resistance was at times
heroic: more often it was merely pathetic. Some 20,000 men
of the East Pakistan Rifles and the East Bengal Regiment
went over *en masse* to the cause of Bangla Desh. But they
were neither well-trained nor well-organized, and certainly
not well-armed. Most later deserted. They lacked seasoned
commanders. They had almost no weapons: a handful of
Chinese automatic guns, a few hundred bolt-action .303 rifles,
a hodgepodge of other ancient gear, and precious little ammunition for any of it. There were, too, the civilians who
joined the resistance, hundreds of Bengali men, young and
old, whose strength was not in the bamboo poles and home-
made spears which were their only weapons, nor in their military skill, for there was none of that, but in their unshakable
belief in the justice of their cause. Some were men who had
seen their families die; many had seen their towns and villages
torn and excoriated by waves of carefully brutalized West
Pakistanis. These were the Bengalis, soldiers and civilians,
who formed the "Mukti Fouj," or "liberation army."

In the early days, it was never an army in any military
sense. It merely comprised bands of desperate, often bewil-
dered fighters, cut off from one another in isolated pockets,
operating against the army in uncoordinated disarray, easily
picked off one by one as the army fanned out from Dacca
into the further reaches of the province. They were sustained,
for a time, by the broadcasts of the clandestine "Radio Bangla
Desh." Soon after darkness fell on March 25, the voice of
Sheikh Mujibur Rahman came faintly through on a wave-
length close to the official Pakistan Radio. In what must have

been, and sounded like, a prerecorded message, the Sheikh proclaimed East Pakistan to be the People's Republic of Bangla Desh. He called on Bengalis to go underground, to reorganize, and to attack the "invaders." And he claimed to be "as free as Bangla Desh"—a tragically true claim, for he was in prison. But it was a claim which fired the resolve of the Mukti Fouj in those early, fraught weeks before they succumbed to the legions of the West. Radio Bangla Desh continued to broadcast, but its claims grew wilder and lost credibility. It soon became obvious that it was not even located in Bangla Desh, but in India.

By the middle of April, almost all the key towns of Bangla Desh were in the army's hold. Only along the West Bengal border, and in the northeast corner of the province around Sylhet, did resistance flicker. There was savage fighting in Sylhet itself—a deserted city inhabited only by old cripples, dead dogs, and carrion crows. The last town to go under was Chuadanga, early on proclaimed as the provisional capital of Bangla Desh, six miles from the Indian frontier. "Resistance" flourished here but collapsed as soon as the army ripped through the town. The mouthpiece of that purely verbal "resistance" was a Dr. Ashabul Haq, a diminutive but handsome fifty-year-old medico who styled himself "Head of the Mukti Fouj," claimed to be in daily touch with Sheikh Mujib, donned a holster and two loaded pistols, and strutted like a turkey for the benefit of foreign television. "We will not have to fire a single shot. Chuadanga will be a death trap for the army," he boasted emptily. For a few days, the doctor was able to pose as the heir apparent of Sheikh Mujib. His pathetic little bid to carve a niche in history ended in bathos, when the army, at a time of its own choosing, mopped up Chuadanga as part of two days' work. The role played by the ridiculous Dr. Haq had in itself no importance, but it served as a bizarre symbol of how easily the Bengalis could romanticize their way out of their problems. These are habits that die hard and are being agonizingly unlearned today in the hard crucible of national struggle. All along, the Bengali leadership lived in and acted out the policies of Cloud-Cuckoo-Land. They either saw what was coming and shrug-shoul-

deredly let it come, or pretended it was not coming at all.
They were almost totally unprepared in anything but rhetoric
for the army's onslaught. Yet, they could have been so much
better prepared. Instead of organizing mass rallies and campaigns of civil disobedience (an instrument which worked
against the British but hardly perplexed the Pakistan army),
Awami League activists should have organized an underground, marshaled the hard core of a guerrilla force, devised
some sort of policy for action, laid contingency plans. But
they preferred their dreams.

Nowhere was such wishful thinking more deplorably displayed than in the Indian press, which espoused the Bangla
Desh cause and then did it the maximum possible harm by
utterly misreporting it. Once all foreign journalists had been
expelled from East Pakistan, there remained only one major
source of information, India. Indian reporters were closest to
the news, they had sources across the unsealed border, and as
Bengalis they spoke the same language and had many of the
same aspirations as the people of Bangla Desh. But India's
newspapers took sides. They turned themselves into the voices
of a propaganda as crude and unbelievable as the regurgitated
rubbish of the government-controlled press in Pakistan. The
editorial writers, gleefully reflecting the visceral reactions of
the Indian Ministry of External Affairs, exulted simply in the
discomfiture of a Pakistan faced with mass insurrection in its
East wing. But if this was merely simplistic, it was at least
opinion. It was what the Indian press gave out as "fact" that
amounted to a dereliction of its duty to inform. Day after day,
in defiance not merely of known facts but of reason and con-
sistency, the newspapers persisted in proclaiming great vic-
tories by the "forces" of the Mukti Fouj, the wholesale "cap-
ture" of towns and large areas, massive "defeats" supposedly
suffered by the Pakistan army. One newspaper, one of India's
best, headlined the "news" of Dacca's liberation and the sur-
render of an entire Pakistan division. Until foreign reporters
gradually succeeded in slipping into Bangla Desh and out
again, to report the picture accurately, the Indian press was
the sole source of what should have been authoritative news.
But it made no attempt to be uncommitted. The Indian re-

porters who filled the columns of their newspapers with "news" from Bangla Desh were Bengalis, all politically and emotionally excited by the cause of Bangla Desh nationalism. Ignoring the canons of responsible journalism, they manufactured the "news" to suit their views and as an exercise in wish-fulfillment. Their editors supinely fell in with this and allowed the stuff to be printed. The atmosphere in India thus became one of hysterical make-believe. The Indian parliament, whose proceedings normally bear scant relevance to the real world (not even the unreal real world of India), discussed Bangla Desh in a haze of total fantasy. Foreign correspondents and observers began to point out the inconsistencies in the Indian reports, which now conflicted completely in their falsehoods and exaggerations with the facts that were becoming known from, for example, foreign nationals who were caught by the war and were only now escaping from East Pakistan. But when foreign writers were skeptical, casting doubts on reports that the Mukti Fouj was near to victory, Indian newspapers and politicians angrily accused them of being pro-Pakistani, or in some other way biased. It was a heyday of unreason.

Eventually, the truth slowly began to dawn. In May, the editor of the *Hindustan Times,* a leading Indian daily, felt forced to admit that reporting had been "extravagant," that newspapers—and, significantly, the government radio—had shown "lack of professionalism, uncritical acceptance of unauthenticated reports and an unconscious mood of wish-fulfillment" which had given the public the utterly false impression that a victory for Bangla Desh was imminent. In fact, it was worse even than that: the reports were not only unauthenticated; many were made up. The mood of wish-fulfillment was not only "unconscious"; it was often deliberate. A consequence of this dismal orgy of distortion was a propaganda victory for the Pakistani establishment which might well have been responsible in part for the subsequent international attitude of unconcern over the Bangla Desh problem which India was to find so deplorable. In those first vital weeks, Pakistan was easily able to dismiss the one source of reporting on what was supposed to be happening in Bangla Desh as the arrant nonsense it transparently was.

However, the Indian press has continued, though more mutedly, to indulge its wish-fulfillment. Responsible Indian opinion, even policy-forming opinion, tends to disbelieve unpalatable truths or facts which fail to fit accepted dogma, particularly on anything to do with Pakistan. Indian attitudes toward Pakistan, Indian policies on Pakistan, are in large part determined by irrational impulses. They are based on a hatred for all that Pakistan stands for and has meant. It is important to note this. For today, no less than at the time of Partition—indeed, largely because of Partition—India and Pakistan interreact. What happens in Bangla Desh will depend crucially on what India decides. Although a strong, admirably level-headed leader, Mrs. Indira Gandhi may not be capable of withstanding anti-Pakistan pressures within her country. Opinion in Europe and America must therefore be as wary of Indian views on Bangla Desh and Pakistan as of Pakistan views, tug though they may at radical consciences. With regard to what could become a major world trouble spot, opinion abroad must also beware of uncorroborated information from Indian sources. For that news comes through a series of distorting filters hardly different in effect from the propaganda mills of Pakistan. And those views are actuated by an abiding dismay that the subcontinent was ever partitioned, by a deep-rooted, "gut" antagonism not only to the creation of Pakistan twenty-four years ago but to the fact of its existence today, and by an obsessive, though often unrealized and unformulated, desire to "bring down" or even destroy Pakistan.

So, for all the vivid Indian accounts of unremitting resistance, Chuadanga fell. The "civil war," if that is what it ever was, was over. How tragically symptomatic that it was only on the *following* day, April 17, that six leaders of the Awami League declared that they had formed the first government of the "Independent Sovereign Democratic Republic of Bangla Desh." It was almost as if they were at pains to show the world that they were out of touch, behind the times. The new nation was proclaimed at a ceremony "somewhere in Bangla Desh" —in fact, it was in a mango grove 300 yards from the Indian border near a village renamed, for the occasion, Mujibnagar. Sheikh Mujib—alive or dead at that time, no one present knew—was declared president. Syed Nazrul Islam, a lawyer and country college teacher, became "acting president"; Tajuddin Ahmed, Mujib's "chief of staff" during the civil disobedience campaign, the "prime minister," and Colonel A. G. Osmani, the seniormost Bengali in the army, commanding officer of the Mukti Fouj. Having performed the ceremony within sight of the Indian border, the assemblage scurried back from the insecurity of their "sovereign republic" to the sanctuary of India—and to obscurity. For the ceremony and the proclamation were no longer relevant. The government of Bangla Desh now based itself in the former Pakistan mission in Calcutta, after defection from the Pakistan diplomatic service of the Bengali deputy high commissioner, Mr. M. Hossain Ali, and thenceforth issued disinformation, pious declarations, impassioned denunciations, and pretty postage stamps, purportedly from "Mujibnagar" or "somewhere inside Bangla Desh." But all this was out of date before it began: the belatedness of the independence ceremony was indeed symbolic. Things in Bangla Desh would never—as the generals had imagined— be "normal" again until the soldiers got out, but they would also never—as the Awami Leaguers imagined—be "normal" once they had. For in terms of the new, revolutionary situation the famous Six Points were mere tepid compromises. They were no longer relevant. President Yahya Khan and his hellbent generals had brought to a white heat a militant Bengali nationalism which, understandably, could see nothing but violence as a solution for its intense, manifold, and growing problems. It is into this new and dangerous phase that Bangla Desh is today beginning to pass.

16

GENOCIDE

The nation is proud of the Armed Forces who deserve all its admiration and appreciation. Let us bow down our heads in gratitude to Almighty Allah.—PRESIDENT YAHYA KHAN

The army now held Bangla Desh in a steely grip. It controlled all the towns, thousands of whose terror-stricken people had fled into the countryside, and from the countryside, joined by tens of thousands more, into India, for the villages and fields were no safer from the army's vicious wrath than were the towns. Already, by mid-April, 1,000,000 refugees had gone across. The flow was to continue, unabated and disastrous, throughout the summer, reaching, by October, a staggering, uncountable, and still mushrooming total of beyond twelve million. As well as the towns, the army controlled all strategic points, the airports, the seaports, and the radio. With its far superior fire-power, know-how, organization and preparedness, this was inevitable. The fantasists—some commentators in India—conjured up notions that the monsoon would bog the army down and leave it at the mercy of Bengali harassment. Wrong, pathetically wrong, again. As the months passed, the army's grip remained. It became demonstrably clear that guerrilla resistance, which did flicker here and there into life and later burgeoned into a considerable disruptive force, nevertheless could never in itself be enough to force the army home.

But equally, while Bangla Desh was in the army's *grip,* it could never come under its *control.* It would never be possible for the soldiers to restore to normal a land where they were an alien, oppressing, detested, occupying force outnumbered 1,000 to one, isolated in cantonments thousands of miles from home, themselves afraid in their isolation and in the knowledge of the Bengalis' searing hatred for them.

The generals, of course, had not planned it this way. But for reasons we have seen, it was inevitable that they should get it wrong. The four or so top generals of the military junta, among whom President Yahya Khan was simply *primus inter pares,* were intellectually blinkered by narrow Islamic and anti-Indian dogma, imbued with a prejudice against the dark-skinned and supposedly feckless Bengalis as crude as any Afrikaaner's for his Kaffir. Ayub Khan made the elite's contempt explicit in 1954, when he was General Officer Commanding in East Pakistan. "East Bengalis," he wrote, "probably belong to the very original Indian races. It is no exaggeration to say that up to the creation of Pakistan, they had not known any real freedom or sovereignty. They have in turn been ruled either by the caste Hindus, Mughals, Pathans, or the British. In addition they have been and still are under considerable cultural and linguistic influence. As such, they have all the inhibitions of down-trodden races and have not yet found it possible psychologically to adjust to the requirements of their new-born freedom."

Some Western commentators have supposed that because professional soldiers everywhere tend to be the duller members of the family—the bright boys go into business or politics— the officers of the junta were unintelligent as well as bigoted men. But their cleverness is not to be underestimated; to do so is also to underestimate the sheer continuing and determined malevolence of which they have proven themselves capable. For they are, at the same time, ill-lettered, ill-read, mulishly stubborn, implacably imbued, rather like the warlords of feudal Japan, with notions that they are the very embodiment of the national (and in this case Islamic) spirit, which finds its expression in an aggressive militarism. They are, above all, staggeringly—and deliberately—ignorant of the nation they lead and certainly of the situation and the people in East Pakistan. And it was this ignorance which helped impel them into error and disaster.

Although president, Yahya Khan is not the most powerful member of the junta. For a time, its leader was undoubtedly General Tikka Khan himself, an advocate and practitioner in past campaigns of terror methods. He is known as the "Butcher of Baluchistan" but in Bengal he excelled even himself. (Tikka Khan, now aged fifty-four, is of humble stock. He was born in a mud hut near Rawalpindi. He was soon spotted by the British as top-caliber officer material, and proved a brilliant soldier, especially as a tactician. But he has always suffered from some kind of inferiority complex over his origins, has never mastered English, and is only barely handy with a knife and fork. These antecedents and deficiencies perhaps explain in part his exceptional ruthlessness and penchant for self-aggrandizement.) By taking on increasingly dictatorial airs, arrogating to himself almost vice-regal powers, he came near to challenging the authority of the president. As a consequence, a group of top officers, just outside the innermost circle but still influential, led by Lieutenant-General Abdul Khan Niazi, persuaded the president to replace Tikka Khan, who was shunted off to command a corps in the West wing.

He still remains, however, a member of the innermost circle. The junta also includes Major-General Muhammad Akbar Khan, who was head of all-services intelligence and is now a divisional commander; Major-General Gul Hassan, chief of staff; and Major-General Ghulam Omar Khan, in charge of military security. In addition to this rather sinister quartet there is an outer circle of equally senior and almost equally powerful officers, who include General Niazi, Lieutenant-General S. M. G. Pirzada and General Abdul Hamid Khan. These men need to be named, identified, for they assiduously shun the limelight. It is they who bear the prime responsibility for bringing immeasurable suffering to the subcontinent. It is their overweening ignorance and arrogance which has ruined their own nation. They imagined they could "save" Pakistan—their Pakistan—by a systematic extermination of the Bengali leadership and intelligentsia. They imagined that this alone would suffice to subdue the East wing for a generation, their remaining lifetime. They imagined that only a token force would need to stay in East Pakistan. But they failed to calculate, because they lacked the comprehension, the consequences of their policy. They failed to see that no mere "token force" could do the job but that it would need an occupying army of not less than 60,000 men to keep its grip on Bangla Desh, through no means other than an unbridled massacre of Bengalis for which "genocide" has become the only apt (if imprecise) word. This exposes the emptiness of President Yahya's sick claim that "only a handful of people" oppose him. The junta's "policy" (if brute force can be dignified by such a term) has stimulated the rise inside Bangla Desh of an extreme nationalist resistance which will be satisfied by no "political solution" short of outright independence bought by blood.

The generals crassly ignored the warnings they were given. In early March, Vice-Admiral Ahsan, East Pakistan's governor for two years, and General Yakub, commanding all forces there, advised the junta against a "military solution" and were removed from their posts. Now, of course, the generals have no answers to the monstrous problems they have created. There is no way except out. But of the seven deadly sins, pride, the stubbornest pride, is uppermost in men like Yahya Khan. Sooner than lose face, sooner than get out, sooner even than implicitly admit error by attempting to salvage something, if only some shreds of honor, from the wreck, the junta prefers the suicidal course of wreaking destruction upon Bangla Desh, visiting the punishment for their own sins upon the Bengali people.

West Pakistan policy aimed at more than merely the quelling of Bengali resistance, for soldiers brainwashed on a course of Bengali race hate were given their head. Whole villages were burned, hundreds of ordinary peasants shot or killed in more gruesome ways, even children bayoneted before their mothers' eyes and then left to die lingering deaths, girls raped and abducted. The martial-law leaders of Pakistan fully understood what they were doing. They even took pains to see that all this went unreported; foreign journalists were not

permitted to return to East Pakistan for several weeks. Nevertheless, details of the terror campaign did come through, in a
trickle at first and from sources that were not reliable, but
later from foreign newsmen who entered East Pakistan clan-
destinely and from British members of Parliament. Finally,
when President Yahya Khan was shamed into readmitting the
foreign press, the horror stories, the reports of atrocity after
atrocity, the accounts of the army's cruel scorched-earth tac-
tics—all backed up by a mass of circumstantial evidence—
poured out of East Pakistan.

Within a month of the crackdown correspondents who had
managed to find their way into Dacca had reported a half-
dead city, a cowed and frightened population. By mid-May
the government's "image" had suffered so disastrously that its
public-relations advisers felt a carefully arranged tour by foreign correspondents might help restore some "credibility." So
six reporters were invited. They were carefully chosen: none,
significantly, had been to East Pakistan before. The authorities evidently felt they would swallow the official propaganda.
But although the six reporters were carefully watched, and
only after protests were allowed to talk to people undisturbed,
their accounts painted a picture of wanton slaughter and destruction. Maurice Quaintance of Reuters quoted an authoritative estimate of over 300,000 dead. People spoke in whispers
and looked over their shoulders before answering questions.
Quaintance found evidence of indiscriminate killing by the
army. He quoted a senior officer at Khulna who said: "It took
me five days to get control of this area. We killed everyone
who came our way. We never bothered to count the bodies."

The government excuse, thought up a week later, was that
killings and intimidation of non-Bengalis in East Pakistan had
reached such a pitch that the army had had to step in to restore order. This was later amplified into a full-blown exercise
in justification in the previously mentioned "White Paper on
the crisis in East Pakistan," issued in August, 1971, which set
out to prove, largely on the basis of a judicious, and tenden-
tious, selection from newspaper reports, that Sheikh Mujib
and his Awami League had never really sought anything less
than outright independence and so, essentially, were traitors.

The regime further claimed that the army, by stepping in on March 25, preempted by only a few hours a full-scale rebellion and secession, plotted by the Awami League, plus a mutiny in the police and the Bengali units of the army. The White Paper then proceeded to attribute to the Bengalis atrocities committed by the military. This was the "definitive" version of the government's case. There can have been few other instances of a government seeking to justify an entire policy on the basis of a few foreign newspaper cuttings. As for the charge that a rebellion and mutiny were barely "preempted," there is not merely no evidence, but every indication to the contrary: if ever a secessionist movement was ill-prepared, if ever there was no prospect of any organized rebellion, it was in East Pakistan before March 25. It is, of course, true that the autonomist movement in East Pakistan growingly took on the character of a secessionist movement and it is also true that, at first, extremist elements sought to create their "state" within the state and, then, that Sheikh Mujib himself, under a variety of mounting pressures, set up a form of parallel government. But the White Paper went well beyond conspiracy. And, even if those charges were true, they could hardly justify what detailed reports soon exposed as a campaign of the crudest, cruelest suppression and a colonization operation unparalleled in its brutality since the Belgian occupation of the Congo in the 1880s.

As to the charges of Bengali atrocities—the gangster element in the Awami League and outside it had run amok. As already noted, a rampant xenophobia ran through Bangla Desh as the emotions of a long-pent-up Bengali nationalism welled to the surface. While in the most public parts of Dacca Bengalis merely destroyed English language signs and non-Bengali shops, in more secluded places they attacked Punjabis and even Biharis—refugees from India who came after Partition. They hacked them to death, burnt them alive, cut their throats—men, women, and chidren unsparingly. At Mymensingh, a postmaster showed journalists his bayonet wounds. He claimed to be one of only twenty-five survivors out of 5,000 non-Bengalis who fell to the knives and hatred of Bengali mobs. In April, Anthony Mascarenhas, a leading

Karachi journalist who was later to leave Pakistan to give the
full story that government censors would not allow him to
write, reported that as many as 100,000 non-Bengalis might
have been slaughtered. He quoted eyewitness stories of rape,
torture, and eye-gouging, public floggings of men and women,
limbs wrenched off, women's breasts severed before the victims were killed. Special brutalities were reserved for Punjabis, Mascarenhas reported. "At Chittagong, the colonel
commanding the military academy was killed while his wife,
eight months pregnant, was raped and bayoneted in the abdomen. . . . An officer was flayed alive. His two sons were
beheaded and his wife was bayoneted in the abdomen and left
to die with her son's head placed on her naked body. The
bodies of many young girls have been found with Bangla
Desh flagsticks protruding from their wombs." From elsewhere there were reports of mothers being forced to drink the
blood of their murdered children.

Because of the strictest censorship, hardly anyone in West
Pakistan knew this, or knew the rest of the story of what was
happening in the East wing. Mascarenhas gave the official
government reason for this: fearful of reprisals against Bengalis in West Pakistan, the government had blacked out all
news of what Bengalis had done to Punjabis in the East.

But the real reasons for the blackout were, of course, quite
otherwise. (The most damning evidence of this was subsequently be provided by none other than Mascarenhas himself.)
It was nonsense to argue that the censorship of the press was
intended to safeguard the Bengali minority in West Pakistan.
This was tantamount to the martial-law regime claiming that it
was unable to uphold its own law and order—which would
have been absurd. While it was true that inept Awami League
leadership forced the Bengalis into desperate courses, in which
hoodlums were encouraged to go on the rampage, there was no
evidence at all that their killings and torturings went to the extent claimed by the apologists of West Pakistan. None of it
came to the notice of the many foreign journalists who were in
Dacca until March 25. The "White Paper," replete with
"evidence" culled from foreign newspapers, could cite not one
despatch from Dacca before March 25 to substantiate its

charges that the Bengalis, not the army, were the first to un-
leash terrorism. The foreign press corps did learn of, and report, the harassment, arson, and looting to which Biharis and
Punjabis were subjected, but this, though deplorable, was
much smaller beer.

So the key question arises, in considering the Pakistan government's claim: *when,* exactly, did the Bengali mob go totally berserk? All the evidence suggests that it was not before,
but *after,* the army's intervention. It is true, of course, that
3,000 were killed in riots before the army waded in, but by
the local standards that were to become current, even this
was a small matter. It was the army that triggered off the real
reign of terror. President Yahya Khan's administration has
totally failed to clear itself of this charge, and the facts cited
in its own White Paper implicitly admit it: most of the incidents it cites occurred, on its own admission, after March 26.
Even less convincing, if that were possible, have been its repeated pleas that all the massacres of the following months
were committed by the Bengalis, that ever "undisciplined,"
"volatile," "headstrong," "Hinduized" rabble which aroused
such contempt in President Yahya Khan and stirs all the ugly,
confused emotions of archetypal race hatred in Pakistan's
leadership today.

It was Anthony Mascarenhas, hitherto regarded as firmly
committed to the government's cause, who utterly exposed
the falsity of the official line. When he had put out the government case earlier, it had been under duress or, at least, under
restraint. Writing in the London *Sunday Times* (June 13,
1971), Mascarenhas shattered that case in a remarkable,
highly detailed factual report which has since been amply
confirmed in equal detail. He recounted exactly how the West
Pakistan army launched a systematic massacre of tens of thousands of Bengalis throughout East Pakistan. He described the
fate of Abdul Bari, a twenty-four-year-old Bengali who had
made the fatal mistake of running within sight of a Pakistani
patrol. Mascarenhas saw him picked up. "Normally we would
have killed him as he ran," the patrol's officer chattily explained. "But we are checking him out for your sake. You are
new here and I can see you have a squeamish stomach." "Why

kill him?" Mascarenhas asked. "Because he *might* be a Hindu, or he *might* be a rebel." (My emphasis—D.L.) Even if such unfortunate men passed the first test (they could easily prove their religion, for Muslim men are circumcised) they obviously stood precious little chance of escaping summary execution on the second.

Mascarenhas described the army's campaign as a "pogrom." Its victims, he said, were not only the Hindus of Bangla Desh, but also many thousands of Bengali Muslims—students, teachers, politicians, police, and soldiers. Mascarenhas said he was repeatedly told by senior officers that the regime was determined to "cleanse" (another race-hate metaphor) East Pakistan once and for all of the threat of secession, "even if it means killing off two million people and ruling the province as a colony for thirty years." Mascarenhas went on: "The West Pakistan army in East Bengal is doing exactly that with a terrifying thoroughness."

He wrote of Hindus hunted down, shot off-hand, and bludgeoned to death, of truckloads of human targets hauled off "for disposal," of whole villages devastated by "kill and burn missions," of brave talk in the officers' mess at night: "How many did you get?" He quoted Colonel Naim, of 9th Division headquarters in Comilla, who claimed a "sort-out" was needed to prevent a Hindu takeover of Bengali commerce and culture, and Major Bashir of the same unit who said the Bengali Muslims were "Hindus at heart" and that this was a war between the pure and the impure (the word Pakistan, in Urdu, means "Land of the Pure"). "Everywhere I found officers and men fashioning imaginative garments of justification from the fabric of their own prejudices. . . . The Punjabis, whose ambitions and interests have dominated government policies since the founding of Pakistan in 1947, would brook no erosion of their power. The army backed them up. Officials privately justify what has been done as a retaliation for the massacre of non-Bengalis before the army moved in. But events suggest that the pogrom was not the result of a spontaneous or undisciplined action. It was planned." Mascarenhas stated that when the army fanned out on March 26, they carried lists of people to be liquidated. It was, he said, "genocide conducted with amazing casualness," in which death sentences were handed out with the flicks of a pencil. In the lush spring fertility of the area around Comilla, one of the most crowded areas of the world, with a population density of 1,900 people to the square mile, "only man was nowhere to be seen." And after much detailed description of the careful terrorization of the Bengali people, Mascarenhas concluded: "East Bengal is being colonized. . . . The first consideration of the army has been and still is the obliteration of every trace of separatism in East Bengal. This proposition is upheld by the continuing slaughter; . . . the decision was coldly taken up by the military leaders and they are going through with it. . . ."

West Pakistan's overstrained and underpowered propaganda machine made futile efforts to shove aside the mass of detail in Mascarenhas's courageous report—a report it was safe for him to publish only after bringing his wife and family out of Pakistan. The regime was even reduced to the smear that Mascarenhas had been "bought." But these efforts were nothing compared with the growing mass of evidence from other sources that showed that Mascarenhas had been right. In its desperate attempts to patch together the smithereens of its reputation, the regime found an attractive ally in Mrs. Jill Knight, M.P. for Edgbaston, whose reports in June for the *Daily Telegraph* were of astonishing naiveté. Mrs. Knight's first account reported favorably a conversation with President Yahya which had convinced her, she said, that he was "no Hitler." He also convinced her that he had given no orders for "rule by mailed fist." Mrs. Knight then went off on a tour (accompanied) of East Pakistan, where she was "unable" to find any evidence of massacres and came away "convinced" (again) that the people who had fled need not be afraid to return. Mrs. Knight's brief venture into investigative reporting was so confuted by the mass of contrary evidence that it barely merits consideration, except for the fact that it confused a lot of people. On her own admission, she spoke mainly to her own countrymen: "I was astonished how much you can find out if you talk to the top people," she told the *Sunday*

Telegraph, in what seemed like a parody of a backwoods Tory
gentlewoman. It would seem that Mrs. Knight was simply
overawed by the olde-worlde pukkah-sahib gentility of President Yahya Khan, whose considerable charm was certainly
turned on to the utmost. A clue to this appeared in a letter to
The Times from Mr. James Tinn, another member of Parliament, who accompanied Mrs. Knight. He wrote: "I was
frankly impressed by Yahya Khan's personality but even more
so by his record of deeds up to the breakdown of talks."

The ridiculous episode of Mrs. Knight had one useful consequence. The president met her request to allow journalists a
free hand again in East Pakistan. This was not a matter of his
succumbing to her charms as she so evidently had for his.
There were good reasons now for allowing the journalists
back. First, as the attempt to bottle up the truth had lamentably failed, the regime had nothing further to gain by continued secrecy, and more to lose: there was a danger of
increasingly antagonizing the Western powers, whose support
might be more than ever needed now that China (Pakistan's
only major ally) was moving toward a deal with the United
States. Secondly, and more important, Pakistan now had an
interest in enlarging the area of tension and world knowledge
of it. The more the world became aware of the deepening crisis
in Bengal, East and West, as the refugee figures soared and the
guerrilla movement, aided and abetted by India, moved up
from first to second gear, the more international pressure
would mount not only on Pakistan but also on India. The
Pakistan aim now became to embroil India, to shift the onus
of blame for the situation onto India. Pakistan sought to raise
tension to an international plane and distort the entire focus
of international attention from what was going on inside
East Pakistan, which was the crux of the matter, to what
was going on along and across the Indian borders. This
accounts both for continued Pakistani requests for United
Nations observers and for consistent Indian refusal to admit
them. If the Pakistanis calculated that allowing the journalists
their heads would bring much "bad publicity," they also
doubtless reasoned that it hardly mattered any more and that
international policies would be no more than marginally

affected by public opinion. And they were right. Meanwhile, the routine denials could continue to go out for consumption by those who cared or chose to swallow them.

So the details of a bloodbath more methodical, planned, and ruthlessly executed than any in modern times since the Nazis now came out in endless spate. Everything that Anthony Mascarenhas had written was multiplied a hundredfold. Indiscriminate slaying of Bengalis was shown to be a commonplace. No less horrible, but more sinister, was the institution of Gestapo-like methods, the "elimination" of "suspects" or "potential subversives," the brutal rounding up and interrogation of professional Bengalis, the establishment of concentration camps in the military cantonments of Dacca, Chittagong, Jessore and Comilla, purposeless torturing, unbridled looting, community punishment, and systematized rape. Whole areas of the town of Khulna were burned down in an operation officially described as "slum clearance": at times, the river was choked with corpses. Soldiers at Santihar destroyed almost the entire town and shot every Bengali they could find, on sight. At refugee camps in India, there are Pakistani babies that have been bayoneted. At Kushtia, Punjabi soldiers raided the house of a businessman and killed all but one (left for dead) of a family of seven. At a village in the east of the province, soldiers murdered two children before their mother's eyes and then shot her as she held the baby. John Hastings, a Methodist missionary in Calcutta, says he has certain evidence that soldiers threw babies in the air and caught them on bayonets and killed girls by thrusting bayonets into their vaginas. At Haluaghat village, volunteer Bengali blood donors were drained of all their blood until they died: the incident, attested to by three neutral Western observers, was cited in the government White Paper as an example of a Bengali atrocity said to have been committed at Chittagong. At Brahmanbaria, entire blocks of streets were systematically destroyed and elsewhere carefully selected houses singled out for destruction. Throughout Bangla Desh, Bengalis feared for their lives if seen speaking to journalists. But enough still dared speak, and the visible evidence of scorched-earth terror was too widespread to be concealed, too evident to be

denied. Another British M.P., Mr. Reg Prentice, wrote in the
New Statesman: "Everywhere we saw the symptoms of a
country in the grip of fear."

A second party of parliamentarians, of whom Mr. Prentice
was one, went to rather more pains than the egregious Mrs.
Knight to find the facts. Nor were they so mesmerized by
President Yahya Khan. Mr. Arthur Bottomley, a former
Labour minister, said it was clear that the Pakistan army had
indulged in mass destruction and killing. Whole areas were
devastated. "Ordinary people cannot cause such devastation
without massive weaponry," he said. Mr. Toby Jessel, a
Conservative M.P., agreed. The army had behaved in an
"utterly uncivilized" way, had gone far beyond what could
reasonably be thought necessary to restore order. The soldiers
were conducting a blitz against the Hindus: "The army is
trigger-happy and arbitrary."

The British delegation's comments were brushed aside by
the Pakistan government as "hearsay." Mounting criticism
in Britian was said to be motivated by British concern for
investments in the tea estates of West Bengal and Assam.
That such rejoinders could be produced at all was a measure
of the feebleness of the Pakistan case. There was even less of
an answer to detailed reports from experts of the International
Bank for Reconstruction and Development (World Bank),
suppressed for "diplomatic reasons" but fortunately "leaked."
Mr. Hendrick van der Heijden (who has no shares in British
tea estates) toured the region for the World Bank. He said
that around Jessore whole villages had been destroyed, half
the town's shops had been destroyed. The city's center and
"some 20,000 people were killed. Generally, the army
terrorizes the population." At Khulna there was similar destruction. Both cities had been totally deserted by their women
and children and no one came out after dark. The town of
Mangla "has been virtually obliterated." At Kushtia, Mr. van
der Heijden reported, army punitive action lasted twelve days
and left the town destroyed and almost deserted. The population was down from 40,000 to 5,000. "Ninety per cent
of the houses, shops, banks, and other buildings were totally
destroyed. The city looked like a Second World War German

town that had undergone strategic bombing attacks. People were sitting around dazed. When we moved around, everyone fled. It was like the morning after a nuclear attack. . . . I asked [officials] to show me a shop where food was being sold: it was in the next ninety minutes impossible to find one. Kushtia is the My Lai of the West Pakistan army. The farmers are not coming to the cities and nobody goes out. Thousands of farmers have fled. Everything is abnormal there and it was a shattering experience." Another section of the World Bank report further stated: "There is no question that punitive measures by the military are continuing and, whether directed at the general population or at particular elements, it is having the effect of fostering fear among the population at large." Insurgent activity was continuing and was inviting "massive army retaliation." Parliamentarians, journalists, and other visitors found repeated evidence of this: scores of villages were razed in such retaliatory action.

On July 30, in Karachi, President Yahya Khan gave his first televised press conference since his nation went insane. Everything was normal in East Pakistan, he said. Those who had fled from "Awami League terror" could quite safely return. The still unceasing streams of people that journalists had seen day after day moving into India were "a show" put on by the Indians. Reports of destroyed villages were "a load of rubbish." "Just that?" the president was asked. "Yes, just that."

17

A NATION RAVAGED

The greatest service of the army of the old Reich was that, in a time of the general "counting by majority" of the heads, it put the heads above the majority.—HITLER

But it was more than "punishment," more than terror, more even than a bloodbath. In fact, it went beyond even "colonization." For at least colonization, however brutally accomplished, can assume some measure of paternal care and some measure of concern, self-interested though it may be, for the condition of the colonized and the effective working of the economy. What West Pakistan has done to Bangla Desh (and it must be called Bangla Desh, for its people, however crushed, will never again acquiesce in its being East Pakistan) is nothing short of a subjugation such as has not been seen since the Nazi occupation of Europe. Bangla Desh has become a Gestapo state. Its people and its towns are shattered. Its economy is paralyzed. And this in an area which was already a continuing disaster.

By the time this book is published, the number of refugees to have fled to India will probably exceed twelve million. Official totals, whether for deaths in war and catastrophe, or lives momentarily salvaged, cannot keep pace with the real numbers. "Establishment" circles in West Pakistan see this new and vast refugee problem as the one "bonus" in the situation, for it heaps a tremendous burden upon India. The cost to the Indian economy, only marginally alleviated by extra foreign aid, is not beyond its capacity to withstand, but it will make serious inroads into India's already faltering efforts to combat poverty and backwardness. Millions of extra people now have to be fed, yet India is already short of food (despite official figures to the contrary). In the pullulating conditions of the refugee camps, epidemic disease, though so far kept under control by an impressively organized Indian relief effort, could break out at any time. Some 300,000 children under the age of five are officially described as "at death's door" from malnutrition. Increasingly desperate as they must be, the refugees themselves could break out, bringing simmering communal tension in an already turbulent West Bengal and an already lawless Calcutta to the boil.

The refugees cannot be resettled in India: Calcutta, with 8 million people, is already in itself a vast camp for refugees unsettled since the days of Partition. The refugees cannot go back. Pakistan's propagandists maintain that reception centers for returning refugees are busy, contradicting their president, who now claims that there are no refugees at all. But those reception centers visited by journalists and others have been almost empty, and no one passes through. The refugees cannot return because they will face almost certain persecution, possible starvation, and the risk of violent death. They cannot return because there is nothing to go back to. Those who owned land would find that it had been auctioned off in their absence by the martial-law authorities. The irrepressibly gullible Jill Knight faithfully recounted in the *Daily Telegraph* that Sultan Muhammad Khan, whose position in name more than fact is foreign minister of Pakistan, told her that refugee property in East Pakistan was being maintained and the safety of abandoned homes was "guaranteed." "I have been assured," she reported blithely, "that President Yahya Khan's statement on welcoming back refugees applies to all who have fled into India . . . irrespective of religion." The nonsense of this is that those who fled into India largely did so precisely because of their religion. And in fact, and in a very organized way, property of refugee Hindus, homes, farms, shops, crops, and other assets, is simply being handed out to their religious and political enemies. There are well-documented cases of it. A house in Comilla which belonged to a fleeing Hindu businessman has been taken over by a senior army officer for his own home. Nearby, the contents of a Hindu-owned pharmacy were being taken off by soldiers as an officer moved in. In Sylhet, Muslims have been able to buy up Hindu homes for nominal sums. In Dacca, too, abandoned houses have been for the taking. In the surrounding countryside, crops and fields have been distributed to government supporters as rewards for loyalty. The fact is that no Hindu who has struggled across into India—ill, maybe, and dazed and faced with appalling problems, but still alive—will now return to Bangla Desh.

The Yahya regime's onslaught against Hindus was symbolized by the pulling down, on July 23, of Dacca's most famous Hindu temple. The anti-Hindu terror has perhaps been the most carefully planned part of the entire subjugation campaign. It has, first, given the army a cause, the moral justification for its war against the Bengalis. The soldiers, unable to distinguish at sight between the Muslim Bengali and the Hindu Bengali and fed, anyway, with notions that one is as bad as the other, see the massacre as part of a morally "cleansing" *jihad,* or "holy war" on the Prophet Muhammad's behalf. Secondly, that *jihad* has performed for Pakistan's leaders the famous old trick which worked so well, though in less extreme form, for the former British Raj: "communally divide and politically rule." By exciting communal animosity in East Pakistan, the army has set Hindu Bengali against Muslim Bengali. Its aim has been to weaken, and if possible to split, the cause of Bengali nationalism. This could well serve the "useful" purpose of sparking communal outbreaks of violence in India. But whether it does so or not, the fact now is that no rational Bengali will or can return to Bangla Desh. Moreover, no Hindu Bengali will ever return there, even if it achieves independence. For the moderate, secular policies of Sheikh Mujibur Rahman, which cemented over communal conflicts, have now gone. The deep springs of communal antagonism have again turned bitter. There is, significantly,

no Hindu member of the Bangla Desh "cabinet" now shel-
tering in Calcutta.

The West Pakistan junta has saddled itself with a policy of
"solving" its East-wing problem "once and for all." Its first
aim has been to crush and stun the people into submission, to
hold the province down by rule of fear. But it is going on
from that into a more sophisticated phase. It has brought West
Pakistanis over in large numbers to run Bangla Desh. It has
begun a policy of "Islamization of the masses," unlovely new
jargon for eliminating separatist ideas, forging a strong, supposedly religious bond between the two wings, sequestering
Hindu property and distributing it as a "golden carrot" to
win over the long-exploited, underprivileged Muslim Bengali
lower middle class.

The deliberate aim is to shatter the social fabric of Bangla
Desh. Leading professionals and businessmen have been interned, perhaps murdered, many of them community leaders
who never took part in political activity. Scores of Bengali
government officials have disappeared in a Stalin-like purge,
to be replaced by West Pakistanis. There has been a mass
enforced drafting of West-wing civil servants to create a
wholly non-Bengali administration, down to the lowest levels.
Bengalis have also been replaced in hundreds of other key
jobs: even the Dacca taxi drivers are now Urdu-speaking. Of
course, many Bengalis have been replaced because they have
simply fled. But this is a consequence of deliberate government
policy: whole stretches of the most overcrowded areas on
earth appeared deserted because people are hiding in terror.
And where the army has eased off, the Muslim League, the
most bigoted and authoritarian of the old political parties,
almost the Muslim equivalent of the Ku Klux Klan, has taken
over the job of repression, not stopping short at burning
Hindu homes. The government has set up a network of so-
called "Peace Committees," whose job is to restore "normalcy"
in East Pakistan. It has recruited several thousand *razakars,*
militant volunteers, to man these committees: mostly thugs,
bigots, sadists, and score-settlers. They come mainly from the
ranks of disaffected small-town elements and minor politicians

who were routed by the Awami League. Those who are not the most hardline Muslim bigots are hoodlums, bullies, and informers who have been given a free hand to impose their own reign of particular viciousness on the people. They have been trained to shoot. The one criterion on which they have been chosen is "loyalty" to the regime. Society has been turned on its head, with the criminal classes in charge.

Thus, a region which is chronically in need of better administration has been brought to a condition of chaos. The population is scared and estranged. The civil service, on which so much depends in a traditionally bureaucratic structure, is under strength, defeated before it begins by the accumulated problems, and speaking an alien language. The army, which from the beginning was the only well-organized body in the country, the only body really up to the task of running it, has alienated the people by abusing its power. In many areas, even now, martinet commanders persist in harassment and persecution. In some places, better officers have sought to win back the sullen populace by more lenient, constructive methods, helping to repair damaged homes and encouraging the tending of crops. But the army is overstretched. It now has not only the responsibility of policing the entire area, and largely administering it, but also of defending the 1,350-mile border with India. It has to face the growing problem of guerrilla insurgency. It is too much to expect that the army, whatever its abilities, can salvage anything out of the wreckage its leaders have recklessly created.

Yet, so long as Bangla Desh remains an imprisoned satrapy of West Pakistan, no one except the army can keep things going. But how to keep going a country which at the same time is in a stranglehold? Administration is impotent. Only the army can get vital stocks of food now rotting at the docks at Chittagong, the only deepwater port, distributed to where they are most needed. Only army reports to Islamabad can obtain the extra grains from abroad which are always needed in Bangla Desh, yet local officers are afraid or reluctant to report how bad the situation really is. Boats loaded with grain have been turned away from Chittagong. Only the army can get the waterways, ferries, roads, and railways open and working again but, increasingly overworked and demoralized, it cannot do so. It has itself requisitioned trucks and barges which are vitally needed to distribute essential commodities. And the population is not co-operating. Hundreds of barges lie idle along the riverbanks. Guerrillas are blowing up road and rail bridges. Chittagong dockworkers have deserted. The railways are almost at a standstill. Many of the skilled and semiskilled have gone. So, in this area where it is quite normal for hundreds, often thousands, to die annually from malnutrition and its attendant diseases, famine and epidemic have been made a certainty. For Bangla Desh was probably less able than any area in the world to withstand a major setback, let alone the continuing series of punishing blows of the past year. Even in "good" times, it needs more than a million tons of grain imports a year. This year, subjugation and chaos have robbed Bangla Desh of its minor rice crop and the main monsoon crop, and it has paralyzed the distribution of seeds, fertilizers, and fuel as well as the movement of seasonal agricultural labor. Sowing and harvesting have been disrupted by the summer's chaos. Many food stores were destroyed. And in the cyclone area, where 3,000,000 people live, where no agriculture is left at all that can continue unaided, almost all foreign-aided rehabilitation work stopped for months. Although millions have fled to India, this has not greatly eased the food problem, which is one of distribution even more than shortage. The League of Red Cross Societies in Geneva has reported that the situation is likely to be "very, very bad": it is not given to overstatement. Many will avoid actual death from starvation by eating vegetation of various kinds, but this will not save children from the permanent damage that protein deficiency causes in the very young. The almost certain famine also means disease of epidemic magnitude. Even in the refugee camps of India, organized and tended by dozens of highly geared medical and relief teams, starvation and disease are only barely being kept at bay. The situation inside Bangla Desh, much of which will go unreported to the outside world, can thus hardly even be imagined. It has been argued that, given the enormous overpopulation of the area, this is not necessarily a bad thing, that it is foolish to meddle with the few major population regulators still left in the world—limited warfare, famine and plague, that man's concern for prolonging lives and preventing premature deaths is imperiling his survival as a species, and that therefore even such phenomena as the high road-accident rates of developed countries are to be welcomed as a way of keeping population from rising out of control, and thus a famine in a country as overcrowded as Bangla Desh can be seen as a kind of solution. But quite apart from its dubious ethics, this approach ignores the realities its proponents fondly imagine they are so boldly facing. It is not merely a matter of numbers. There are the vast political repercussions in this increasingly sensitive area to consider. If millions of people become convinced that they have nothing left to lose, if continued disaster and neglect deprive them of all stake in the system, there is bound to be a political convulsion of the highest magnitude. And as Lenin pointed out, the shortest route to Paris runs through Calcutta and Peking. It is, if nothing else, simply shortsighted and self-defeating to brush aside the famine and disease problems of remote or unappealing places like Bangla Desh simply because they seem, on a very superficial viewing, to be handy population regulators.

In its attempt to retain economic dominance through political domination, President Yahya Khan's regime has lost both. It has destroyed the very fabric of the economy and society in the East wing. It has also done immense damage to the economy of West Pakistan, which could well lead yet to crucial social stresses. In its devastating indictment of the situation in Bangla Desh (revealingly described as "heresy" by the Pakistan official spokesman), the World Bank team reported in July: "There is no question that punitive measures by the military are continuing . . . which is fostering fear among the population at large. . . . The situation remains very tense and anything but conducive to the resumption of normal activities; . . . there are no signs that normality is being approached or that matters are even moving in that direction or that the situation will improve significantly or rapidly. . . . Commerce has virtually ceased and economic activity generally is at a very low ebb." Bangla Desh jute, mainstay of the economy of all Pakistan, earning half its foreign exchange, has simply rotted in the fields. Jute is a difficult crop, only arduously harvested. It will not be produced in the quantities of the past by an unwilling peasantry militarily held down. It must, further, be skillfully processed, but the mills are hardly working. It must be transported, but there is no transport. It must be exported, but the ports are clogged. Artificial fibers already seriously compete with jute on world markets, and Pakistan as the world's chief supplier is in critical danger of losing its best export potential forever. Further, the occupation of Bangla Desh imposes immense financial strains. The unreckoned and irrecoverable costs of maintaining a large army thousands of miles from home, defending long borders and dealing with insurgency, is debilitating in the extreme. Its currency reserves are exhausted. Development aid from abroad has almost dried up. Even before March 25, prices were spiraling, industry stagnating. The ruination of Bangla Desh has now deprived Pakistan's major manufacturers of their best markets. A whole range of consumer industries in West Pakistan, notably textiles, has been hit hard. Two industries have publicly appealed to the president to save them from collapse. Industrial unrest is mounting as workers are laid off. The government has been forced to resort to deficit financing. It has defaulted on its international debts by means of a so-called "unilateral moratorium." In his broadcast to the nation on June 28, President Yahya himself admitted that the economy was in ruins: "Our exports have sharply declined . . . collection of taxes has suffered . . . we have to use our resources with much greater restraint . . . this involves hardship and sacrifices . . . a thorough revision of the import policy . . . inessential items banned . . . in domestic spending also maximum economy is being exercised . . . modest development program . . . maximum austerity": a grim litany of self-inflicted wounds. China, it is true, has offered to bail Pakistan out—the first installment came in May with an interest-free $211 million loan. But China is not a rich country and cannot afford to prop Pakistan up indefinitely, even if she might wish to do so for political reasons, which is increasingly doubtful. Rarely can a nation's leadership have been so blind, so crass, so utterly unmindful of the inevitable, obvious consequences of rash policies. President Yahya seeks increasing resort in a telltale defensive bluster, but even he has been forced to admit the state of Pakistan's economy to be "so bad I cannot tell you. I inherited a bad economy and I am going to pass it on." Honest, yes; blunt, indeed; and a dreadful confession of abysmal failure.

18

RESISTANCE

If one bullet is fired, build a fortress in every house.—SHEIKH MUJIBUR RAHMAN

In the weeks following his *Anschluss* in Bangla Desh, President Yahya Khan insisted to the world that the situation had reverted to "normal"—though even this would not have been anything to be particularly proud of. One of the many tragedies, though a minor one, in the appalling situation was that he quite possibly believed it. For the regime, ever ignorant of the realities in East Pakistan, had now deliberately cosseted itself in a cocoon of misinformation. Immured in Islamabad, it pulled down the blinds, stopped up its ears, and totally insulated itself from the high-voltage shock of world reaction. In this it was abetted by Pakistan's ambassadors abroad, who "doctored" their reports and made light of worldwide condemnation. And when even this could no longer shut out the flood of censure, the regime found refuge in paranoid delusions which blamed the Hindus and the British, the Jews and the BBC, the Russians and the World Bank, for concocting a giant world conspiracy to blacken its name. But the clear fact was that Bangla Desh could not possibly return to normal as long as it remained a forcibly occupied state. The regime set two target dates, April 21 and (when that failed) June 15, for workers to return to their jobs without prejudice. But the people remain recalcitrant: neither offices nor factories nor workshops are back to "normal." So far from being "normal" was Bangla Desh that by August, for example, it was still unsafe for the president to go there, and a much-heralded visit was canceled.

With surprising speed, a ruthless and determined guerrilla resistance burgeoned inside Bangla Desh. The army had crushed the stuffing out of the political leadership; the peace committees and the strong-arm *razakars* clinched the dictatorship's grip upon the population. Yet the regime could not even begin to bring the region back to normal. It has had to keep the army there, and keep it busy. For the first time in its history, Pakistan has had to introduce conscription, yet the army's massive reinforcement has still proved too little. The three crack divisions are further than ever from attaining real control. By day, the soldiers hold uneasy, superficial sway; at night, Bangla Desh becomes an enclave of the guerrillas. Alongside the soldiers are civilian-clothed toughs of the Pakistan Special Forces, experts in the kind of CIA activity which has been one of the most signal of all the many American failures in Vietnam. Despite an effort which has come near to bankrupting the nation in a matter of months, the army is too preoccupied with internal security to patrol its own borders adequately, let alone defend them in the event of the war which President Yahya has repeatedly threatened to declare against India. This gives the lie to the president's pretense that it is Indian infiltrators who are causing disruption inside Bangla Desh.

The open border, however, does mean that insurgents have a safe haven on the Indian side, a situation very like the Cambodian sanctuaries used by the Vietcong in Vietnam. And this is not the only parallel with Vietnam; Bangla Desh is almost ideal guerrilla warfare country, with its maze of irregular and shifting rivers, streams and waterways, its swamps and jungles, its paddy fields and banana groves and jute fields waist high in water. But it is a matter of more than mere geography. Not for nothing did the Maoist leader Maulana Bashani exhort the peasants to turn Bangla Desh into a new Vietnam. Today it is becoming just that. Control of the Bangla Desh national movement slid from the Awami League at the moment of Mujib's arrest and the flight of its leaders from the people they purported to lead. Their attempt at compromise with what Mujib called the "coteries" of West-wing vested interest had demonstrably failed, as the Left had always predicted. As the Left has always argued, there was no halfway house. The army onslaught of March 25 proved the extremists' points for them, as the sacked Vice-Admiral Ahsan had warned. And so, even by mid-April, hardline Maoists had taken over command of many units of the Mukti Fouj, easily wresting the leadership from ineffectual Awami Leaguers. To them, this was a Vietnam situation, with a peasant people resisting an alien invader in a bid for self-determination. And, as in Vietnam, that alien force was quickly finding that it had stumbled into a bottomless pit. Internal insurgency throughout the summer, even during the monsoon, has increased day by day, at a pace which belies Bengali habit. The Mukti Fouj (Liberation Army) restyled itself the Mukti Bahini (Liberation Forces) as a token of its growing power. The guerrillas have blown up dozens of vital road and rail bridges, disrupting the East-wing economy on which West Pakistan so heavily depends. Guerrillas have put three vital power stations in Dacca out of action and there are several incidents in Dacca every day. They have blown up power lines throughout the province and power plants on the tea estates. Their actions have grown bolder: they caused a major explosion at Dacca's Intercontinental Hotel; at Srinagar, ten miles southwest, they took over the post office, robbed the bank, and locked up the police station. India has given help and sanctuary to the guerrillas, though not as much as President Yahya claims: India has been inhibited by her new treaty with the Soviet Union, ratified in August, which is designed to preserve the *status quo,* and by her fears that undue assistance to the insurgents might force President Yahya into a war. Thus, while giving small arms and ammunition, India has deliberately starved the Mukti Bahini of any medium or larger armament.

The Pakistan army is one of the most professional fighting services in the world. But to the mounting guerrilla campaign in Bangla Desh, it has no effective answer. Soldiers guard the bridges round the clock, government offices and other

vital buildings are sandbagged, but still the bombings continue.
The only way the army can respond—as armies reflexively
respond in such situations—is to step up terror methods. But,
of course, a more counterproductive policy could hardly be
devised. After each guerrilla attack, the army piles in, destroys
the nearest village, and takes off all the men for "questioning."
There could hardly be a better way than this policy of indiscriminate reprisal for recruiting zealots to the Mukti Bahini.
Its hard core numbers only 3–4,000, former members of the
Bengali regiments, the police, and paramilitary organizations.
But these are enough, and anyway their numbers grow daily,
though the inflated estimates put out by their India-based
spokesmen are yet another example of Bengali wish-fulfillment. General Grivas won the guerrilla war in Cyprus with
far fewer men in more difficult terrain; small bands of Vietcong have hamstrung whole divisions of the American army in
Vietnam; years of conflict have failed to quell insurgency in
India's northeastern territories. On any practical assessment,
it would take a force of at least 250,000 men trained in
counterinsurgency operations to counter the Mukti Bahini,
and this is far beyond Pakistan's capacity. The direct cost
alone of maintaining the army is already at least 10 million
rupees ($2,184,000) a day. Although this is about the same
as the cost to India of the refugees, it is eroding Pakistan's
economy. President Yahya's policies are as ruinous as they
are futile.

It was Sheikh Mujibur Rahman, the "traitor," who was
foremost in warning the regime that he was their best, indeed
their only, bulwark against the floodtide of Maoism which
would inevitably swamp East Pakistan once given its chance.
In a land where life is so very cheap, the harshness of a
rampant revolutionary credo is not so unattractive. Indeed,
it can become an inspiration. The weak, idealistic, only
vaguely nationalist philosophizing of the Awami League (in
the very relevant Marxist terminology, a "bourgeois" party),
was too inadequate an ideology to sustain a prolonged guerrilla struggle. Inevitably, the antigovernment leadership
quickly passed to revolutionaries. These were men like Lieutenant Ali, a hard, barefooted irregular who, after March 25,

escaped from jail where, as a political prisoner, he had been viciously flogged, and within a week established himself as the driving force and moral leader of the Bangla Desh resistance movement around Sylhet. Showing me his ragged clothes, he said: "Look at me in these. I have no time for myself. I care only for the people's struggle. There can be no compromise with the enemy. It is all or nothing for us." This man, and there are many like him now who are the mainsprings of the Bangla Desh resistance, will never be coerced or bought. Such men command respect and loyalty, even if they are hard, even if they insist, as they must, on the sternest discipline. Every unavailing effort by the military junta to defeat and destroy them will only toughen the Bengalis' resolve to strive for the national determination which they see as their birthright. And the resistance is more than military too. The extremist groups have found common cause in a new "Liberation Struggle Coordination Committee," which has issued a detailed directive enjoining the setting up in every village of an all-party "People's Liberation Council" to take over the administration, direct village protection forces, and administer justice through "People's Courts." These councils are to see that no taxes are paid, that collaborators are punished, that guerrilla squads are organized and cared for, that the government supply lines and communications are damaged, and that the people are "educated" by the guerrilla squad leaders.

All this makes pitiably irrelevant the Islamabad regime's endeavors to restore the situation to normal. President Yahya continues to protest, too much, that his aim is the "transfer of power." Having crudely thwarted that process once, his attempts to salvage credibility since have been lamentably unconvincing. In yet another nationwide broadcast, on June 28, the president said he had no alternative but to have a constitution prepared by experts. It would take account of national aspirations "as assessed by me." It would come into effect without discussion by the national assembly, and that assembly, which would meet in about three or four months' time, circumstances permitting (which, in fact, they did not), would, in effect, be a handpicked body. The Awami League, of course, would be banned. All its elected members would be screened: some would be allowed to retain their seats, as individuals; others would be debarred and by-elections would be held to fill the vacancies. Later it was announced that only 88 of the 167 Awami League legislators who had been chosen in December would be allowed to sit in the new assembly as independents, and that 59 of those excluded would be put on trial.

This latest broadcast did nothing except confirm the utter intransigence of the president's thinking and policies. Matters had already gone far beyond any hopes of reconciliation. Nevertheless, a more astute or less myopic leader might at least have made the right conciliatory noises. But not Yahya Khan. "The nation is proud of the armed forces, who deserve all its appreciation and admiration," said the president stonily. The troubles in the East wing, he said, were the work of "secessionists, miscreants, rebels, extremists, intruders, anti-state elements, criminals, mischief-mongers, saboteurs, and infiltrators"—the gamut of authoritarian clichés. Sheikh Mujibur Rahman, who was to be put on secret military trial on August 11 without defense counsel of his own choosing, had conceived an "evil design," was "irresponsible" and "un-patriotic." Ritually, the president invoked the hollow shib-boleths of any bankrupt politician, appeals to played-out abstractions: the memory of Jinnah, the founding faith of Islam. Pakistanis, he said, were "people whose life is pulsating with the love of the Holy Prophet, whose hearts are illumined with the light of Iman and who have an unshakable reliance on the help of Almighty Allah." Such cant must have been a comfort to the bayoneted babies of East Bengal.

The president himself found comfort in supposed overseas reaction to his policies. "It is a matter of satisfaction . . . that in the difficult situation that the country has faced in the past few months the reaction and response from an overwhelming number of countries has been one of sympathy and under-standing." This was plumbing the depths all right, but whether of hypocrisy or complacency it was impossible to tell.

It was a tawdry performance. The leader of the nation's largest party was in jail, facing a death sentence, having won a patently unrigged election, having participated in lengthy constitutional discussions, having waited at his home to be arrested and interned, yet now accused of having been in evil league with India to destroy the nation. The Bengalis were now being cheated even of their aspirations by President Yahya, who arrogated to himself the right to decide what they were. Inside Bangla Desh, resistance was mounting, terrorism on the rampage, the poverty of millions exacerbated by disruption, famine imminent, the economy (on the president's admission) in ruins. But: "No sacrifice would be too great to bring back economic stability and *to ensure* the unity of Pakistan."

President Yahya Khan's own policies had lost him the right either to demand or to order those sacrifices, because those policies had irrevocably alienated the country's majority wing. In these circumstances, the president's political proposals were a sham. The most popular party was outlawed. On the president's specific recommendation, by-elections for those who were to be unseated should be contested only by parties "not confined to any specific region"—in other words, a revived Muslim League representing the most illiberal, discredited, and rejected political elements in the nation. Awami Leaguers not unseated would now be in a minority and quite helplessly exposed to persecution if they dared step out of line. A terrified electorate could be counted upon to be compliant at the polls, if an election was ever staged.

And there was little chance even of that. By August, Bangla Desh guerrillas had killed 500 collaborators. The fate awaiting Bengali Quislings was shown in Khulna, when the chairman of the local "peace committee" was beheaded in full daylight at his home, though he had ten armed *razakars* guarding it. Anyone cooperating with the regime to the extent of standing for its counterfeit assembly would obviously risk a similar fate. This is the new mood in what was once East Pakistan. Historical and political compulsions and the pigheaded policies created by them have insured that Bangla Desh can never again be part of Pakistan in any meaningful way.

19

RECKONING

*Even without war, the prospects for humanity are
precarious enough.*—PROFESSOR J. D. BERNAL

Pakistan began, in Jinnah's poignant phrase, "mutilated,
motheaten and truncated." It has ended in the same way. It
hardly stood a chance, with its frail economic base, tattered
social fabric, gimcrack political superstructure, absurd geography, and, most debilitating of all, its synthetic nationhood
based on the chimerical premise that Islam was enough.

Yet, it is there, so split, so ravaged by violent self-contra-
dictions, so torn by internal conflict, that the world at large
could be sucked in. For it has caused an international calamity, bringing more misery to more people than any recent
crisis, Korea, Vietnam, the Middle East, or even Biafra. And
by involving India so directly it has created the possibility of a
war. And if that war were fought, it would be with Russian
arms on the Indian side and Chinese and American ones on
the Pakistani—an index of great-power involvement in the
region. But, apart from war, the world outside cannot be
aloof, for the solution of Pakistan's chronic problems of economic backwardness and political troglodytism has proved
beyond the capacity of her inadequate leaders.

Any chance of Pakistan finding its own way to a political
solution was lost forever in the summer of 1971. Even after
the army campaign to crush resistance, President Yahya Khan

perhaps retained some small chance of piecing together the nation's shattered unity, fragile though it would always have remained. It would have required the most adroit, conciliatory policies. But, as we have seen, President Yahya deliberately threw away the last opportunities by his broadcast of June 28. He had already denied himself almost all room for maneuver. Yet, he could have found a way of releasing Sheikh Mujib and allowing the people of the East wing at least a figment of political liberty. It is, of course, doubtful that this could have worked: the newly forged, extremist nationalism now taking grip of Bangla Desh would not have been appeased. But for a president pledged to defend the "integrity" of his nation, it would (had there been any rational consideration) have been worth a try. The Awami League and many Bengali moderates bitterly oppose a Maoist usurpation of their autonomist movement but the very severity of West Pakistan's suppression has made them powerless to resist it. They might have welcomed some accommodation, however inadequate, if only to staunch the bloodshed. It was, true, almost certainly too late. Perhaps the generals, with a rare flash of realism, saw this. But more likely their ingrained religiose dogmatism and military fanaticism led them to spurn even this slight chance of saving something from the wreckage.

No prospects remain, therefore, of any political solution within the context of a united Pakistan. And this must apply even if the Yahya regime falls. There is some prospect of this happening. There are signs that the generals, as the recriminations multiply, are now differing among themselves. Under pressure, President Yahya Khan replaced General Tikka Khan with a more moderate martial-law administrator, General Niazi, and a puppet civilian governor, Mr. Abdul Motaleb Malik, aged sixty-six, a compliant and superannuated Bengali politician, brought out from retirement for the occasion, whose appointment even Mr. Bhutto felt constrained to dismiss as "eyewash." But even if the junta's resolve does not falter, they have no answers to the problems they have created. They therefore seem almost certain to be squeezed, and perhaps ejected, by the many kinds of mounting pressure within West Pakistan itself. As we have seen, the West

Pakistan economy has been mangled. This has set up acute political strains. Although Pakistan's conflicts did crystallize into an East-West confrontation, neither wing is monolithic. However, in the East wing, Bangla Desh, the bid for nationhood will impose a unity of its own. There is no similar common cause in West Pakistan. While it was significant in December 1970 that the hard core of Mr. Bhutto's support came from the northern districts of the Punjab where the army is recruited, this is not necessarily significant today. Nor is the likelihood that Mr. Bhutto's infamous "Karachi to the Khyber" speech, which precipitated the crisis, was made at the junta's behest. Zulfikar Ali Bhutto is out for political power. It is questionable how long he can tolerate being denied it by the army. A first sign of Bhutto's impatience came as early as July, in a little-noticed interview given to the Teheran newspaper *Kayhan International,* which was heavily censored in Pakistan. The remarks that were censored were, of course, those that were most interesting and significant. Mr. Bhutto said: "The quicker the assembly is convened the better. . . . Things are bad in Pakistan. The terrible situation in the East cannot be without effect on the West. There is the danger that West Pakistan will also be plunged into tragedy if no settlement is reached speedily. Delay in a return to normal civilian rule can be fatal. . . . There should be no attempt at installing a puppet civilian government. . . . I shall destroy such a government through mass movement in less than a month." It is easy to see why Pakistan's master suppressed this revealing interview. But Bhutto was not to be so easily contained. By September he was openly calling in Karachi for an early transfer of power.

The army, however, is in no hurry to relinquish its hegemony. It distrusts Bhutto even as it uses him, distrusts his inconstancies and the "socialism" in his Islamic Socialism. It fears the power of the urban and peasant upsurge which won him a massive vote. There are more crucial strains, too, inside West Pakistan. The protracted colonial war, having lost it its best internal and overseas markets, has caused inflation, unemployment, and scarcities. There is simmering unrest throughout the wing as soldier families are bereaved, as the demands of the underprivileged northwest region continue to be ignored or bypassed, and as economic conditions deteriorate. The generals have certainly not forgotten that the movement which ousted President Ayub and brought Pakistan to the brink of revolution in 1969 began with restiveness in the West wing. There is every reason to suppose that it will again be what happens in West Pakistan that determines the fate of East. A new upsurge in the West wing could bring about the independence of Bangla Desh. From an economic point of view, this would be a better prospect than a war which is as ruinous to West as to East Pakistan, and the extremely powerful "22 families" and other industrial, commercial, and mercantile interests will certainly not allow themselves to be scuppered. Even an independent Bangla Desh would not be without its commercial prospects, despite estrangement from West Pakistan, or so they will argue. So it is pressure in the West wing rather than a straightforward triumph of arms by the Mukti Bahini which is the more likely to bring down the junta.

But this will not, cannot, help toward a political solution of the East-wing problem. And this is so because no change of regime can alter the basic irreconcilables, let alone induce the Bengalis, after all that has happened, after the holocaust of 1971, to let bygones be bygones. The very division of Pakistan into two wings places, in itself, unbearable strains upon its unity. Many states have survived against huge geographical odds, but more often than not those odds have proved too great. Even in small, highly developed countries (like Britain), the regions most distant from the capital and power center (Scotland, Cornwall, Wales) suffer from a sense of deprivation—often justified. For larger national units, as, for example, the United States a hundred years ago or India today, one of the most basic problems is communication, communication in all its senses: links such as the roads and railways, the telephone and telegraph, which assist an integrated economy; the administrative and political links which further national integrity, help reduce misunderstanding among the different regions and help curb, also, the competition among them for possibly scarce resources. In a word: infrastructure.

Then there are the human contacts which assist the cross-fertilization of ideas and encourage the cultural affinities, including a common language, which are the stuff of true nationhood. Pakistan has had none of these vital links. Moreover, it is too poor a country to do much about improving them even if this were (as it has not been) an aim of its governments. Pakistan can never be more than a national unity in form only. No amount of force, no political formula, can eradicate its physical division, and this unalterable separateness produces all the other divisive strains which have rent Pakistan. They have made its nationhood nothing better than an abstraction in the Statesman's Year Book and the unreal world of diplomatic protocol. Thus the much canvassed international prescription, that Pakistan's problems must be and can be politically solved, is so much eyewash. Britain has suspended aid until there is a "political solution" (which can mean anything and nothing). The United States, more cynically, has taken a leaf out of Britain's Biafra book and *not* suspended aid, in the vain pretense that it can thereby "influence" President Yahya to find a "political solution"— which cannot be found because it is not there. India and Russia, hustled by Pakistan's saber-rattling into a mutual defense pact, have uttered the same empty cliché, though clearly, in India's case, through gritted teeth. But they are all chasing chimeras. What "political solution," other than some sham like that foisted on the nation by the president in his June 28 broadcast, can there possibly be? On every count, the two wings of Pakistan have been fundamentally two nations for years. What has happened in 1971 has been, in essence, only the logical outcome of long-set policies and attitudes and facts. Glib formulas cannot change that. To urge "political solutions" is to fall in with the humbug dispensed by Islamabad; it is to accept President Yahya's fraudulent claim that a fair "political solution" is as much his aim now as it ever was, and that it is, even, on the verge of fulfillment.

The question, then, is not whether there can be a "political solution" but whether Bangla Desh can achieve self-determination by the only means open to it, force of arms, and then sustain itself. This is no certainty. Many national movements in modern times have been successfully crushed. The case of Biafra, though different in many key ways from that of Bangla Desh, is not an encouraging augury, and Bangla Desh has neither aroused as much world concern nor received as much outside aid and encouragement as Biafra did, despite its greater significance in terms of the number of suffering people involved, in terms of its crucial geographical position, and in terms of its potential effects on great-power politics. But the resilience and determination of the Bengali resistance is already evident. The extravagant claims of its spokesman can be ignored, but there is independent evidence of its success. With covert Indian aid, and fired by the conviction that its cause is just, the Mukti Bahini has successfully pinned down a far superior Pakistan army and made it impossible for West Pakistan to continue as a mere economic leech. Despite their easygoing nature and their proneness for talk instead of action, the Bengalis have never been so feckless as to be incapable of action when it was called for. They have, in fact, a volatile streak which often disconcerted the British and which has also been one of the sharpest thorns in the flesh of independent India. But the Mukti Bahini will never, of itself, be strong enough to compel the army to withdraw or the regime to yield. The odds against it are too great.

But the collapse of the West-wing military junta for internal West-wing reasons, which we have already considered, could take years. It is likely to take years. Nations like Pakistan, with a predominantly agricultural economic base, can withstand strains far greater and for longer than any "developed" nation. Pakistan on a war footing, disciplined by severe economic retrenchment and all-round austerity, could sustain its military quests in Bangla Desh almost indefinitely, particularly, of course, if it continues to receive injections of military aid from the United States. With India now restrained by Russia through the new mutual-defense treaty, there is little chance that even the immense and unrelievable burden of, say, 10 million refugees could tempt India into seeking to superimpose a military solution of her own. There is thus the real prospect that, as so often in the subcontinent, nothing much will happen at all, the "crisis" will fizzle out, and the situation will simply stagnate, to become just one more of the many chronic problems that beset southern Asia without hope of amelioration or solution.

These, however, are rational calculations. But much of what has happened in Pakistan this year has been wildly irrational. By any normal standards, the generals have lost their heads. They have adopted a policy of lunatic and suicidal overkill. They have shattered their own nation. They show every sign of being blind to the consequences of their actions. There is no reason to suppose that they are incapable of further recklessness. It is significant, therefore, that President Yahya Khan has repeatedly threatened to declare war on India. He has sedulously portrayed India as the real villain: alleged Indian infiltrators, alleged Indian complicity with Sheikh Mujibur Rahman, alleged Indian bases for training Mukti Bahini guerrillas, alleged Indian supplies of arms and ammunition. "I shall declare a general war," the president thundered in July, and many other times. This is, of course, the bluster of a patently defeated man. Secure, responsible leaders are not given to crude threats. But a war could solve many of President Yahya's most pressing problems. It would override the fissiparous pulls which are the most dangerous threat to West Pakistan's stability. It could also invite swift international intervention to stop the fighting, and bring another imposed Tashkent-type settlement. This would well suit Pakistan's book. For another Tashkent would stick to the conventions and, therefore, underwrite the *status quo*. That is, it would confirm and sanctify and give international backing to the vassal status of East Pakistan. It would withhold any form of recognition of the separatist movement in Bangla Desh as an independent national force in its own right. Thus a war could help to pull President Yahya's chestnuts out of the fire by imposing a "political solution" on the combatants. It would completely shift the focus of the crisis, which is essentially a West Pakistan–Bangla Desh issue, and turn it into a West Pakistan–India issue, and the resulting "settlement" would not be an answer to the essential problem. Thus, as the army's position inside Bangla Desh worsens, and as West Pakistan's condition becomes more critical, the chances of President

Yahya precipitating a war with India may grow, even if, as
even he must realize, Pakistan cannot possibly win it. The
spark can be expected not on the eastern side, but along those
same lines in the Punjab or Kashmir where so much blood
has been mercilessly spilled in the years since Partition.

But it is still unlikely that either this, or a coup, or any
change of government, can solve the great range of new
problems which will in future confront West Pakistan. The
East wing can never now be anything but an incubus, militarily, economically, and politically. Yet a Pakistan without
its East wing would be a weakling, delicate, shaky, unstable,
fissile. It is, of course, far-fetched for Indian commentators
to be speculating already about the dismemberment of West
Pakistan: reunifying the Punjab under the Indian flag; "liberating" Pakistan-held Kashmir, apportioning Baluchistan to
Iran, perhaps, and the northwest frontier region to Afghanistan. But it is hard to see that a West Pakistan standing alone
would have much future. The prospects for an independent
Bangla Desh look a little better—though, given its vast problems, not much. However well things went for it, even given
inspired political leadership (of which there is no sign), outside
aid and encouragement (which would come only grudg-
ingly), absence of physical calamity (statistically improb-
able), and as well of new enthusiastic patriotism (faint
prospect), its problems still loom insuperably. But, no longer
sucked dry of its resources and revenue by the West wing
and with its economy no longer distorted by the military ob-
session with "liberating" Kashmir, it could perhaps become
economically viable and at least able to trade again with its
natural commercial partner, West Bengal.

Yet, economically viable or not, the problems of Bangla
Desh, or East Pakistan, or whatever it becomes, have arguably
passed beyond the point of any solution at all. I believe that
what has passed in East Pakistan this summer is essentially
a symptom of a nation out of control, with problems that are
probably beyond the resource and capacity of the human race,
at least at present, to solve. Essentially, these are the problems
of poverty and population. (Mr. Peregrine Worsthorne, of
the *Sunday Telegraph,* with his characteristic flair for medie-

valism both in elegance of style and ethereal vagaries of argument, has put forward a Thomistic view that the agony of Bengal results not from its material but from its moral backwardness. This, to my mind, not only begs the questions but hinders the very attempt to solve, or even identify, the problems.) All that has happened in Pakistan, the tortuous political wrangling, the constitutional maneuvering, the civil war, the refugee exodus, the death and living death brought to multitudes of utterly innocent, ordinary, hapless folk, has been the final expression of two deep-set, chronic problems. Poverty and population are not peculiar to Pakistan. They are more than just the economic or political difficulties that beset all developing countries. They are more even than the problems which have hit Pakistan particularly hard because of its physical division and other special features. They are global problems because they have gone beyond national or regional ability to solve. What answer is there to the question of how to cure, year in, year out, the abject poverty which kills thousands annually from starvation and disease, the poverty which means that millions are without a home and never, simply never, have a proper meal? What cure is there for the illiteracy and degradation which that same poverty creates, which saps the human spirit of the mass and inflames the righteous fury of the few into nihilistic extremisms? What solution to a population problem which adds nearly 3,000,000 people every year to East Pakistan's congested riverlands and which has produced an overcrowding so intense that 3,000,000 people have no choice but to live on the unprotected sandbars of the Ganges delta in the well-beaten path of death-dealing cyclones and tidal waves? How to counteract the implacable opposition of Islam to birth control? Indeed, how to control the births even in theory? Are there, can there be, solutions to such problems? In three years of asking every available expert in such subjects as agriculture, water control, population control, nutrition, social planning, economics, anthropology, and even morals, specialists in every discipline from the most particular to the most general, I have met no one who has even the glimmerings of an answer that is more than a palliative. That is the position of East Pakistan, or Bangla Desh, today.

This has immense implications for the world as a whole. In Pakistan, Russia and America compete for influence and both compete with China, Pakistan's closest present ally. Because of China's links with Pakistan, Russia has forged tighter links with India. Because of the deep-rooted enmity between Pakistan and India at all times, because of the re-percussions of the Bangla Desh crisis upon India at the present time, there is a constant threat to peace in the region. Its strategic position is crucial—to the north it is between the great land mass of Russia and China; to the south it borders the Indian Ocean with its vital military and commercial links between both these continents and Africa where, again, the great powers are competing for influence. In southern Asia, four of the five largest nations on earth meet. Thus, the world powers are inescapably involved.

The Nixon administration has chosen to underwrite the martial law regime with continued supplies of American arms, in defiance of public and even congressional opinion. Pakistan, of course, did the United States a "favor" by facilitating Mr. Kissinger's secret trip to Peking in July. But this does not make the United States, as its apologists have pleaded, be-holden to President Yahya: there are ways to Peking other than through Rawalpindi. American policy seems to be based on the premise that the devil you know is better than two you don't—that a Pakistan "united" under President Yahya Khan is better than an independent West Pakistan and an independent Bangla Desh. But facts are facts, and the "unity" of Pakistan is no longer a fact, if it ever was. It is surprising that the American government has not learned the lesson of Vietnam, that military hardware does not work political miracles.

China's position, of course, is even more inscrutable. But China's present support for the military junta is certainly not immutable. Peking would be quite capable, indeed, of giving covert aid to the Bangla Desh resistance while continuing to back the Yahya Khan regime. Peking needs to have con-tinuing influence in the subcontinent, chiefly as a counter to

growing Russian involvement with India, and is therefore
likely to side with the regime in Islamabad, whether it is a
"reactionary" military clique or not. For the time being, China
has had to subordinate ideological considerations. At the same
time, it is hard to see how Peking can, by its own lights, stay
aloof from a peasant "liberation" movement in Bangla Desh,
so like the one led in China by Mao Tse-tung himself. Growing Chinese involvement, therefore, also seems inevitable.

Both Russia and the United States are concerned that if
the Pakistan mess leads to a war, it could create a fertile field
for mischief-making by China and other nations. But there
is an even greater, longer-term danger. While avoiding outright war, whole areas of the subcontinent could collapse
into a dangerously unstable anarchy, or go into even deeper
economic decline. The acid test is Bengal. Today, an international frontier cuts through Bengal, which was divided on
communal lines in 1947. Yet, even as Muslims hate Hindus,
they are conscious of their brotherhood as Bengalis. Lord
Curzon, the great British Viceroy, divided Bengal in 1905
but the government of India was compelled to reunite it six
years later. Now, today, the wave of Bengali national consciousness which has swept through Bangla Desh has also
touched India's Bengalis on the western side of the frontier.
It is most significant that the Marxist extremists of West
Bengal, like the Awami League, have formulated their own
version of the Six Points. In Calcutta, a vast and ghoulish
refugee camp in itself, a collapsed, anarchic city in which
civilization has visibly been beaten, there is a seedbed for a
rampant, violent communism, or any other "ism." Not only
extremists but even the moderates there believe that their
city and their province is exploited and neglected by an un-
caring, rapacious, and distant central government, nearly
1,000 miles away in New Delhi. This is the Dacca-Islamabad
syndrome! The Naxalites, the extreme, underground com-
munists of West Bengal, are in close contact with the Mukti
Bahini. Clearly their aim is not merely the Bangla Desh of
East Bengal but the Bangla Desh of all Bengal. This has been
dismissed as the "figment of foreign journalists' imaginations"
and so, for the moment, it is. But it is also the figment of

Naxalite and Mukti Bahini imaginations, which is far more significant. Once an independent Bangla Desh is a reality, or even if Bangla Desh fails to attain its independence but becomes instead that "second Vietnam," then West Bengal, on the very doorstep, is ripe to be drawn in. Its problems and its needs are so similar. India would fight as ruthlessly as West Pakistan has done to prevent the secession of its major industrial state. It is therefore not surprising that Mrs. Gandhi, India's prime minister, has resisted nationwide demands to recognize Bangla Desh. For President Yahya Khan's problems could all too easily become her problems—not this year, or next, perhaps not even for a generation, for the time scale on the Indian subcontinent is not a Western one, and change comes slowly. But it is evident that what has already happened in Bangla Desh in a few, fateful months has radically transformed the entire power balance in this part of Asia. Bangla Desh is only one violent symptom of a great political sea-change which is surging across all of South Asia. In less than one year, between June 1970 and March 1971, the peoples of Ceylon, Pakistan, and India all voted overwhelmingly for new, radical solutions (even if the parties and personalities they voted for were unlikely or unable to give them), and in Ceylon, Pakistan erupted angrily into revolt. The people of this crucial region, totaling nearly 700 million, have served clear notice that they are no longer the patient, docile, sloe-eyed and slow-moving, ambitionless, content, ineffectual, and dependable "boys" and "babus" who so eased the white man's burden, but are restless and impatient for change.

So the tragedy of Pakistan could yet turn into a vaster tragedy. The many problems of Bangla Desh, which, in my view, have probably gone beyond the point where there is any solution to them, are only the problems of India in more concentrated and dramatic form and there is no reason to suppose that India too will not face days of similar reckoning. For India's undoubted economic and agricultural progress is only barely keeping pace with rising population and quickening aspirations. So the problems of Bangla Desh and Pakistan are not isolated. Yet almost every world leader, U Thant, President Nixon, Sir Alec Douglas-Home, Mr.

Podgorny, even Mrs. Gandhi, and of course President Yahya
Khan, all dispense that Utopian nostrum, a "political solution." The trade union of nation-states is for the *status quo*
at almost any cost. Like any trade union, it sticks to the rigid
closed-shop rules. Hence the open backing given by the United
States to President Yahya Khan, a policy of unspeakable
cynicism. One would have thought that quite apart from
being disastrous, the Pakistan military government's policies
have been so savage as to be unworthy of any civilized
nation's support. But nations, of course, are not in the morals
business. As the United States, Russia, and China, and India,
all see it, the "political solution" which maintains the *status
quo,* even if it means the repression of the eighth largest
nation on earth, is to be preferred if it seems to produce some
short-term peace and stability in southern Asia. But this is to
see the world in blinkers. This very stolidity of attitude is
itself a basic reason why the problems of Bangla Desh *have*
passed the point of no return. Of course, the major powers
rightly abhor "Balkanization," but as the two halves of
Pakistan have never really been a unity, the problem of
"Balkanization" does not arise if they divide. Pakistan has
always been a fiction, a nonsense, a nonnation which other
nations have gone on pretending is a nation. This has enabled
them to indulge for a generation in a studied, wishful disregard of immense problems which have been beyond Pakistan's capacity to solve. Now, through that disregard, they
have probably gone even beyond international capacity.

This is not mere defeatism. It is not logically necessary
that problems have solutions. Man's ingenuity is not provenly
limitless. If in fact these problems have gone beyond solution,
then the crisis of Bangla Desh could have the profoundest
long-term consequences. Yet, even these may prove beyond
international capacity to appreciate, let alone act upon. For
nations, international communities and civilizations, like individuals, do not always act rationally, do not even always
seek self-preservation. The forms of community escapism are
legion.

But if people and nations do care, and they need to, they
must first recognize that Pakistan is not an island. Pakistan's

very existence is a world problem which touches every nation. And the condition of that existence and the possible termination of existence are also world concerns. Basic to this is an understanding of the current crisis. It has been my thesis that the many basic flaws in Pakistan's make-up only precipitated, but did not create, this crisis; that they only exacerbated, but did not create, the fundamental problems.

These, I believe, are the problems of poverty and population. I know of no solution to them. I know of no approach to a solution to them. If it is true that they are the crux, pat political solutions will not serve. Distant nations will find no solace in their distance. "Joi Bangla" will prove no mere nationalist chant, but the future's lament.

POSTSCRIPT

As anticipated, all-out war between India and Pakistan, smoldering with mounting intensity throughout the summer, eventually erupted on December 3, 1971. As this postscript is written, in mid-December, Indian armies are on the roads to Dacca, and the West Pakistan army, cut off by land, sea and air, is retiring desperately into the three major cantonments it still holds at Dacca, Comilla and Chittagong, having relinquished Jessore and Sylhet without a fight, for a last ditch stand before the inevitable annihilation or humiliation. And "Bangla Desh," formally recognized by India on December 6, is on the way to becoming a reality. Pakistan's crisis has thus proved to be its final, possibly its mortal, crisis, for Pakistan as created by Jinnah can never be the same, or even half the same, again.

As the monsoon petered out in October, after extensive flooding which added to the miseries of the refugees in West Bengal, Mukti Bahini guerillas stepped up their internal offensive. This, of course, could not have been achieved without increasingly evident Indian collusion and assistance in arms, training, sanctuary, the provision of "advisers" and, in the last stages, outright intervention by the Indian army. To record this is not to detract from the innate strength of the resistance movement or its basic justification. The alienation of Pakistan's East Wing from its western exploiter was completed by President Yahya and the junta on March 25, 1971, and the dread-

ful days that followed. From then on, it was merely a matter
of time before East Pakistan's independence became a fact.
Without Indian help, this might have taken many years.
(India's role in this process was akin to that of France in the
achievement of American independence in 1776.) In the upshot, it has proved a matter of months, and there seems no way
now in which Bangla Desh can ever rejoin Pakistan.

During the summer and autumn of 1971, the terrible realities of the situation wrought by their insensate policies pain-
fully dawned on the Islamabad regime. As a symptom of this,
the decision-making process in the capital crumbled. Governmental responsibility, in all senses, disintegrated. President
Yahya Khan declined into the escapism of an undisguised
debauchee. Administration lost all sense of direction, purpose,
method.

In desperation, President Yahya was to announce yet
another face-saving scheme, devised on American advice,
promulgating a new constitution and the transfer of power to
civilian government by the end of December. With the Awami
League still outlawed and its leader, Sheikh Mujibur Rahman,
still in solitary confinement, this could be nothing better than
a sham—which was clearly demonstrated when by-elections
for seats "vacated" by banned Awami Leaguers were held and
most were filled by Muslim Leaguers without a contest.

On December 7, three days after the destroyer *Shah Jehan*
was sunk in a naval battle off Karachi, President Yahya
finally announced the formation of his civilian government.
By then his armies in East Pakistan faced a debacle and his
nation, split in two, had exploded. Ironically, this was the
very time, when, if ever, an embattled nation could justifiably
claim to need a military leadership. President Yahya's appointment as Prime Minister was Mr. Nurul Amin, eighty-three, a
played-out "has-been" who had won a year before one of the
two East Wing seats which did not go to the Awami League.
Mr. Bhutto was named as his deputy and foreign minister, and
a civilian cabinet was formed. Yahya Khan remained President
and retained, of course, the real levers of power, declining
though that power now was. All these gestures were too late to
save Pakistan's situation, and even had they not been, they were

politically bankrupt. Any pretensions to democracy were a fraud and a mockery.

What compulsions and inducements determined President Richard Nixon's choice to side so devotedly with the Islamabad junta remain, at this stage, inexplicable. The White House itself, at any rate, has not explained. In the last days before all-out war, India did, it is true, seem bent on provoking Pakistan beyond the limits that any self-respecting nation could be expected to endure. Growing Indian interference in Bangla Desh, still at that time Pakistani territory, was aggression in any normal sense of the word. Indian attempts to portray it as "self-defense" were Orwellian "double speak" and were delivered with all of India's customarily grating sanctimoniousness and sham piety. But the fundamental fact remained: Indian policy was a response to the crisis, not its cause. The root cause, as India correctly insisted, was the military suppression of the Bengali autonomist, and later secessionist, movement. That led directly to the influx of nearly ten million refugees into India, a number which, after doubting and deriding it, Islamabad finally admitted. That influx, seen in New Delhi as a form of aggression in itself, set up intolerable strains in India's eastern regions. Of these, the obvious economic ones were not the most important, huge though they were—as if, analogously, ten million people had suddenly descended on California. There were the even more dangerous social, communal and political strains, all mounting dangerously, which fueled New Delhi's anxiety. After Mrs. Ghandi's trip to European capitals and particularly to Washington (where President Nixon found it expedient to speak about the weather!!!!!!!), India saw no way out except to force the issue. Even so, the weight of evidence suggests that it was Pakistan which started the war on the western front. But even if it were India, the root cause lies in the disastrous policies adopted by President Yahya and his men, encouraged and bolstered by President Nixon, for reasons that have not been proffered but which can be presumed to have been most cynical—to the dismay not merely of millions of Asians, but many of his own countrymen, too.

The future, as this book goes to press, is disturbingly uncertain. The unresolved Indo-Pakistan war seems sure, whoever wins (and maybe no one wins such wars), to end in the dismemberment of Pakistan. But once, somehow, the peace is achieved, there will still loom ahead the awesome problems of Bangla Desh, marginally improved perhaps by independence, but in many ways exacerbated by the traumas of 1971: a nation torn and devastated, liable to be rent by violent political schism between moderates and left-extremists, a nation liable to be pathetically dependent on India or some other patron, a nation inescapably hobbled by its wretched basic problems. West Pakistan, too, will now face the task of finding a new identity, a new morale, some new sense of national purpose. The danger there could easily be that this task will prove too great, and that there will then be further wracking spasms which will convulse the subcontinent, carrying always the risks of wider war, spelling always anguish and misery for its hapless, innocent millions.

About the Author

David Loshak, who has been staff correspondent for the London *Daily Telegraph* and *Sun Telegraph* in India and Pakistan since March 1969 is one of the few Western observers who has known Pakistan and the surrounding area intimately throughout this key period.

Born in London thirty-eight years ago, he became a journalist after leaving Oxford, where he took honors in Modern History. He has had wide experience as a foreign correspondent. Among his assignments have been the civil war in Nigeria, the Six-day War in the Middle East, and the Cambodian crisis of 1970.

Mr. Loshak is married and the father of two children.